YOU'RE NOT ENOUGH
(AND THAT'S OKAY)

YOU'RE NOT ENOUGH
(AND THAT'S OKAY)

Escaping the Toxic Culture of Self-Love

ALLIE BETH STUCKEY

SENTINEL

SENTINEL
An imprint of Penguin Random House LLC
penguinrandomhouse.com

Most Sentinel books are available at a discount when purchased in quantity for sales
promotions or corporate use. Special editions, which include personalized covers,
excerpts, and corporate imprints, can be created when purchased in large quantities.
For more information, please call (212) 572-2232 or email specialmarkets@
penguinrandomhouse.com. Your local bookstore can also assist with discounted
bulk purchases using the Penguin Random House corporate Business-to-Business
program. For assistance in locating a participating retailer, email
B2B@penguinrandomhouse.com.

ISBN 9780593083840 (hardcover)
ISBN 9780593083857 (ebook)

Printed in the United States of America
3 5 7 9 10 8 6 4 2

Book design by Ellen Cipriano

This book is dedicated to my husband, whose belief in me changed my life, and to our daughter, our precious gift.

CONTENTS

YOU'RE NOT ENOUGH (AND THAT'S OKAY)

INTRODUCTION

When I was seven, I explored the idea of following in Britney Spears's footsteps. My parents wouldn't let me buy her CDs ("Is she asking someone to *hit* her??"), but I'd heard enough of her music at friends' houses to know that I wanted to do what she did. I'd spend hours in my room after school practicing my singing and choreographing routines to whatever I had playing in my boom box. I was sure I had what it took.

As you can probably guess, things didn't go that way. It turns out you actually have to be able to sing and dance to be a singer and a dancer. I eventually faced the harsh reality that I would never have what it takes to rock a red leather jumpsuit and a high pony in a music video. It was hard, but I coped.

I'd guess you have a similar story. You had your own wild aspirations, only to one day confront the realization that Tyra Banks wasn't going to discover you at the mall while you were shopping at American Eagle with your mom and ask you to be on the next season of *America's Next Top Model*.

We're all stunningly confident as children. We've yet to become fully self-conscious, and we have little concept of the potential for failure. So we declare our aspirations, unafraid of embarrassment or the possibility that they won't come to fruition. This self-assurance is part of the wonderful charm of kids. As we grow, it necessarily fades as we start the natural process of reconciling our plans with our actual potential.

I want you to imagine for a moment what it would be like if we *didn't* go through that process. What if we clung to the out-of-the-realm-of-possibility dreams we had as kids and spent our lives pursuing them, no matter the consequences? I'd be selling EPs of my latest acoustic cover of "Toxic" on Instagram and you'd still be learning how to smize in your mirror at your parents' house. It wouldn't be pretty.

As we get older, we're supposed to tell ourselves hard things. We're supposed to grow up, assess our strengths, do things we don't want to do, and realize we're not as special as we think we are. We're supposed to get out of our houses, get over ourselves, and create a life that's productive and meaningful. The confidence we have in ourselves should change from juvenile blind adoration to grounded awareness.

A truth that we all come to terms with at some point in our adolescence is that we don't have what it takes for one thing or another. In other words, we're not enough. We don't have enough talent, a high enough IQ, enough coordination, or enough facial symmetry to do the thing we were sure we would end up doing. Facing our inadequacies is crucial for appropriate development.

And so I find it silly—and downright dangerous—that we women are fed this phrase so constantly today: "You are enough." The vast network of lifestyle bloggers, motivational speakers, fitness gurus, and spiritual Sherpas who live on our phones relay this message daily. We are enough for our kids, enough for our job, enough for our husband, enough for God, enough for ourselves. There's nothing that needs to be added or taken away, we hear. We are perfect the way we are.

We know it's not true. We realized this early on when we abandoned our dreams of pop stardom, and, in a different way, we realize it today. Just like I wasn't enough to be the next Britney, I'm not enough to fulfill other roles either, even though they're real. I'm not enough to be all the things I need to be at once: a good mom, a successful writer, a present wife, a solid friend, a faithful Christian. It's just as crazy for me to think I'm enough for these things as it was for you to want to be a five-foot-two runway model. This time, it's not just about talent. We may have the abilities to do most of these things well. It's also about capacity.

We don't have enough time or energy to be all that we need to be for the world around us. And when we don't measure up to our or others' standards, we drown in the dregs of self-loathing and insecurity. To numb the pain, we open Instagram, scroll for a few minutes, then click on our favorite self-help blogger and check her latest post, which reads "You are enough."

Ahh. Balm for the weary heart. We're flooded with warm feelings of gratitude as we read her caption reminding us that we're strong, powerful, capable women whose dreams matter and whose stretch marks are beautiful and who are so much *more* than just moms to needy kids and wives to needy husbands and are perfect and wonderful just the way we are. "SO true," we think to ourselves. "I am!"

We're comforted, but only for a moment. The next second, when we look at the monitor and see our supposed-to-be-sleeping toddler wiggling just minutes after we've put him down, or remember that we have about fifteen pages left on the assignment due tomorrow, or look in the mirror and hate the body we see, our feelings of self-assurance quickly fade.

Many of us find ourselves in this cycle daily: feeling burned out, seeking encouragement from superficial sources, then feeling better only to feel worse a few hours later. This is exactly the consequence of getting sucked into what I call the toxic culture of self-love.

The culture of self-love tells us that we are enough. And that until we love ourselves into realizing our enough-ness, nothing in our lives will be right. We're told a lack of self-love is why we haven't started that company we've been thinking about. It's why we're settling for the guy we don't really want to be with. It's why we haven't lost the weight or bought the car or done the thing we've been dreaming of doing. Because we have low self-esteem, struggle with self-doubt, and can't kick this addictive habit of self-criticism, we're unable to live the lives we were meant to live.

Dancer and actress Julianne Hough put it this way: "I think every girl needs to love herself, regardless of anything. Like, if you're having a bad day, if you don't like your hair, if you don't have the best family situation, whatever, you have to love yourself and you can't do anything until you love yourself first." All of our successes, the thinking goes, depend on self-love.

I host a podcast called *Relatable*, where we analyze culture, news, and theology from a Christian perspective. Two years ago, a listener asked me to do an episode on what the Bible has to say about self-love. At that point, I had no idea the term was so popular. I was familiar with self-help, and I knew women were being fed a message of self-empowerment and independence, but I didn't know how integral the idea of loving yourself had become to our cultural dialogue.

I quickly found through my research that self-love has been a hot topic for decades. Nearly a half century of psychology has focused on high self-esteem as the solution for society's problems—from academic failure to crime. This made me wonder: If self-love isn't a new phenomenon, if we've been taught for decades that our lives will be made better just by loving ourselves more and feeling confident, why hasn't it caught on? Why aren't we all happier?

In fact, it seems we're *less* happy than ever before. Americans under forty are more depressed, anxious, lonely, and suicidal than any generation before us. We report stronger feelings of purposelessness than any other generation too. We are isolated and unsure of what we want to do with our lives. Many of us feel empty.

And it's not for lack of self-focus. Most of us have been the centers of our own universe for as long as we can remember. Our most prized possessions all have the letter *i* in front of their names. We're the generations of "about me" sections, personal profiles, and selfies. We are well acquainted with instant gratification, and we've come to expect the ability to personalize our experiences. We are keenly focused on ourselves and our needs. We spend hours studying our signs and personality types in an effort to gain the self-understanding we hope will bring us guidance and inner peace. Unlike our parents and grandparents, we are endlessly committed to finding careers we want rather than taking the jobs we need. We are the "everybody gets a trophy" generations, who were often given awards just for showing up. In general, our lives, for better and for worse, have revolved around us.

When it comes to committing to something bigger than ourselves, many of us would rather not. A 2019 Pew Research poll found that millennials make up the largest number of religious "nones" in America, falling far behind our predecessors in affiliation with Christianity.* An NBC / *Wall Street Journal* study from the same year found that young Americans are far less likely than older generations to care about faith, family, and patriotism.

We've spent our lives prioritizing ourselves, our wants, and our happiness, and, guess what. *We're still not happy.* So

---

*Becka A. Alper, "Why America's 'Nones' Don't Identify with a Religion," in Pew Research Center's Fact Tank, August 18, 2018, https://www.pewresearch.org/fact-tank/2018/08/08/why-americas-nones-dont-identify-with-a-religion/.

how in the world could it be that self-love is the answer to our problems when there's no evidence whatsoever that we've ever stopped loving ourselves?

These are the questions I considered as I studied the pervasiveness of the culture of self-love. And I started to wonder: Maybe our happiness doesn't stem from the fact that we don't love ourselves enough. Maybe we're unfulfilled, lonely, and purposeless because we love ourselves *way too much*. Yes, many of us struggle with insecurities and even self-loathing. But these are just other indicators of self-obsession. Even when we don't like ourselves, our perpetual prioritization of our wants, needs, problems, and dreams above all else proves that we still love ourselves a whole lot.

A couple of months into my research, I came across a video on my feed for Hillsong Church, where Hailey Baldwin Bieber gave a testimony of her faith. In it, she said, "I think that every person has had that feeling that they are not enough for something, someone . . . but . . . you are, because God took his time to create [you] and put you in this place."

That's it, I thought. That's the essential lie young women are believing in this culture of self-love. Young Christian women, even. The lie that "you are enough."

The idea that you're enough is central to the culture of

self-love. The logic goes: because you are complete, perfect, and sufficient on your own, you don't need anyone else to love you to be content. All you need is yourself.

I totally get the appeal of this thinking. It's true that we obsess over others' approval and acceptance. We become distracted and detached from things that matter, like our families, friendships, and jobs. Instead of fulfilling our roles well, we're stuck focusing on what roles other people have and how well they're filling them. It's also true that we shouldn't fully depend on others for our happiness or allow their approval to define us. Acknowledging these things, it feels right to comfort ourselves with the mantra "I am enough." And because I am enough, we may tell ourselves, all I need is my own love to be secure and successful.

But here's the thing: our sufficiency isn't the answer to insecurity, and self-love isn't the antidote to our feelings of self-loathing.

Why? Because the self can't be both the problem and the solution. If our problem is that we're insecure or unfulfilled, we're not going be able to find the antidote to these things in the same place our insecurities and fear are coming from.

Our self-love isn't enough to make us confident. Our self-sufficiency isn't enough to bring us peace. Our self-care, self-empowerment, self-help, self-*whatever* are only going to give us so many good vibes before we move on to the next self-betterment program. The self isn't enough—period.

The answer to the purposelessness and hollowness we feel is found not in us but outside of us. The solutions to our problems and pain aren't found in self-love, but in God's love.

The God who created us, who created the universe, who is the same yesterday, today, and forever, is the one who provides us with the purpose and satisfaction we're seeking. While self-love depletes, God's love for us doesn't. He showed us his love by sending Jesus to die for our sins so that we could be forgiven and live forever with him. Self-love is superficial and temporary. God's love is profound and eternal.

And his love compels us to something much better than self-obsession: self-sacrifice. While the thought of putting others before ourselves is considered blasphemy in the culture of self-love, it's the joyous mode of operation for those who follow God. God's love frees and empowers us to consider and serve other people before and instead of ourselves.

This is an argument I made in a podcast episode titled "Three Myths Christian Women Believe." The first myth was that you are enough. My counter was this: you're not enough, you'll never be enough, and that's okay, because God is.

I highlighted this passage from Ephesians: "And you were

dead in the trespasses and sins in which you once walked. . . . But God, being rich in mercy, because of the great love with which he loved us . . . made us alive together with Christ—by grace you have been saved." We are corrupted, helpless, and spiritually dead on our own, *but God*, through *his* power, saves us, sanctifies us, and makes us alive in Christ. We are less than "not enough"; on our own, we're nothing. But God.

The episode resonated. To my surprise, there were thousands of women who'd bought into this and other common lies without even knowing it. The day after it was published, a listener wrote to me in an email:

"I have struggled my whole life with self-hatred. It came from multiple places: my broken home as a child, my need to be successful for attention . . . the list goes on. I became a Christian in college, and since then I have read countless books by Christian authors trying to tell me how to 'fix' it and be 'enough.' The messages all kind of stayed the same: that I just needed to love myself more, because Jesus loved me, and that I was enough. . . . Your podcast opened my eyes. Who knew all I needed to hear was, 'You're not enough, you will never be enough, BUT GOD'?"

Similar messages flooded my inbox. I realized then that the culture of self-love and its central lie that you are enough wasn't just a subject in a viral video or a blog post. It's a mind-set that's plaguing many of us.

And a lot of young women are looking for an alternative. For good reason: the culture of self-love is exhausting. While we're telling ourselves we're enough as we are, we're also reading the next book, listening to the next podcast, or following the next ten-step plan to help us realize and manifest our enough-ness by finding our "best selves." But if we were really enough as is, we wouldn't have to try so hard to convince ourselves it's true.

We're looking for that one method or mantra that's going to show us how to use self-love as the key to unlock our inner treasure box of talent and success. But every time we try, the lock changes. Today we think meditation will get us there. Tomorrow, crystals. Next week, organizing our closet. The week after that, cutting out processed foods. And if none of that works, then we look for a new book or podcast to give us the latest, greatest self-love strategy that we're sure, this time, will help us finally achieve our truest self and help us live our best life.

We're addicted to the thrill of it. It's exciting to think that *this* shift in thinking could really be the game changer.

But the fleeting excitement is overwhelmed by disappointment. None of our methods work long term. No amount of yoga or sage burning or energy shifts or personality tests or essential oils or closet organizing or food prepping or booty exercises or whatever else the self-love stars say you need to finally, truly, be happy with yourself will ever convince you that you're enough. Because you're not. Neither am I. And that's okay.

I want to make this clear upfront: when I talk about the damaging effects of self-love or the emptiness of self-care, I'm not encouraging self-deprecation or shame over getting our nails done. This book is about why the world's answers to our very real feelings of self-doubt, self-loathing, incompetence, and insecurity aren't sufficient and how God's solutions are better.

This book is about *good news*. While the admission that self-love won't satisfy us may feel counterintuitive (it's certainly countercultural), it also gives us immense relief. We get to remove this crushing burden of trying to muster up a love inside us that just doesn't hold up under the weight of life's demands. We get to rely on a sovereign God to be our sufficiency, our confidence, our guide, and our giver of purpose.

This book is about dismantling the lies the toxic culture of self-love has fed to us and replacing them with God's truth. We'll dig into these five myths:

1. You are enough.
2. You determine your truth.
3. You're perfect the way you are.
4. You're entitled to your dreams.
5. You can't love others until you love yourself.

You've heard these popular mantras propagated in the world of self-love, and while they sound inspirational on the surface, they lead only to confusion and desperation. Just like leaving some of our childhood dreams required us to confront hard truths about ourselves, accepting our limitations today will require us to take some tough-to-swallow pills. As we do, the mirage of self-sufficiency will fade, and along with it, the false hopes "you are enough" promises. Any time we let go of a false hope and replace it with a hope that's real, we grow up a little bit. That's what this book aims to do: to help us grow up by replacing the empty hope we have in ourselves with the satisfying hope we can place in God.

I learned how to do this the hard way.

MYTH #1

YOU ARE ENOUGH

I WANTED TO BE ENOUGH

"You're going to die," she told me, leaning forward on the edge of her seat. Her elbows rested on her knees, and her hands were clasped as if in prayer. "This is going to kill you."

I knew I had a problem, but I didn't want to admit it was serious. I just couldn't kick the habit of throwing up my meals. What started out as restricting my calories and working out twice a day turned into a cycle of bingeing and purging that, as hard as I'd tried, I couldn't get out of.

It had started to affect my life. I'd be at a restaurant, having just finished dinner and unable to enjoy the conversation with my friends because I was thinking about how badly I wanted to get rid of the food I'd just eaten. Once, when I was working at a conference for work, I lied to my coworker about needing to get something out of my room so I could go throw up. Another time a friend caught me in the bathroom, my head over the toilet. I thought she was downstairs. She walked in and asked if I was okay. I said I was fine. She didn't push, but she knew I was lying.

I wanted to stop. It was embarrassing. It was inconvenient.

More than that, it wasn't who I wanted to be. I'd never struggled with any kind of addiction. Before that year, I had never gone to extreme lengths to lose weight. But here I was, in a counselor's office, hearing that what I was doing was killing me.

About a year earlier, I'd been through a bad breakup. I dated a guy for two and a half years who met all my criteria: a Christian from a good family with solid friends and a nice personality. We met my freshman year, and I thought for sure he was the one. But things got rocky two years in, and both of us were having doubts. But I was determined to hang on because I was convinced I couldn't find anyone better.

The fall of my senior year he broke up with me. Though I was devastated, I knew I didn't want to spend my last semester sad. So I rebounded—but not in a good way.

I started going out more often and drinking more heavily. Single for the first time in my college career, I had a slew of new dating prospects. I was hanging out with people I considered the "party" crowd. They welcomed me and encouraged me to live it up these few months before the last year of college ended. The newness of it all helped numb my pain.

I also restricted the calories I consumed and spent multiple hours a day working out. The more weight I lost, the more alcohol I drank, and the more guys who paid attention to me, the easier it was for me to ignore the haunting fear the breakup had left me with: that I wasn't enough.

Things got worse. Eventually I missed food too much to keep skipping meals, so I started to eat again, only to throw up an hour later. At first it was just once or twice a week. Then it became an addiction I just couldn't break. I'd started to binge. When I did, I'd feel guilty and afraid I would lose all the "progress" I'd made, so I'd get rid of the food as quickly as I could.

Fast-forward to a few months after I graduated from college, and I was in a new city in a new job, and I was stuck in the same cycle. I was still going through guys and drinking too much, and I was still throwing up my meals. But I started to feel like I could no longer keep up with my own addiction, and, honestly, I was getting a little worried. I'd thought I had the power to turn it all off after the semester ended, but I didn't. This "season" was turning into my actual life. It was one thing to me to have some college "fun," but I wasn't okay with this behavior becoming *who I was*.

So one morning at work I called a number I'd found on a list of recommended Christian counselors on a local church website. I thought the process would be simple: I'd get a few tips on how to live a better life and some mantras or mind games that would break this binge-and-purge addiction.

I believed that because that's the popular message today: you already have everything you need inside you to solve your problems. The idea that while outside tools like therapy, medication, meditation, yoga, hypnosis, or crystals can help unlock your innate potential for health and happiness, you are ultimately healed by the inner power you naturally possess. But this isn't reality.

Rarely does *Teen Vogue* publish helpful articles, but in July 2019 its site published an insightful op-ed critiquing modern wellness culture titled "Being Diagnosed with a Chronic Illness Taught Me That Health Isn't a Meritocracy." The author wrote:

"Women have been conditioned to believe both that our bodies are our self-worth and that our bodies are under our own control. As wellness culture would have us believe, health is a meritocracy in which 'fueling' your body and 'detoxing' and holding crystals can rocket you to the top."

Her debilitating fibromyalgia showed her that no amount of self-care could completely heal her, and that the road to coping with her sickness was going to mean dependence on others rather than self-sufficiency. She realized that healing, whether mental or physical, isn't a quick fix accomplished by unleashing our inner power.

We're not enough to heal ourselves. I don't mean that natural remedies and positive thinking aren't at all effective; I'm saying that we don't have some inherent mystical force inside of us ready to solve our life problems or physical maladies.

I learned the same lesson in my counselor's office. Though I reached out to her because I knew I needed help, when we started, I thought the process would be one of self-empowerment. I figured she'd give me the keys, and I'd unlock my own capabilities to stop overdrinking, ditch the unhealthy relationships, and quit the bingeing and purging.

I was a product of the mainstream messages of our day. Though my mess of a semester should have taught me that "doing me" led to a dead end, I didn't want to give up control and I didn't want to decenter myself from my world. I still wanted to believe I was enough.

But the counseling sessions weren't as straightforward or as focused on self-empowerment as I would have liked. At first the counselor just listened. Then over the course of a few weeks, she helped me peel back the layers of defensiveness and delusion I'd used to bury the sting of rejection and fear of loneliness. She helped me see that underneath all my behavior was my crippling fear of insufficiency. The attention I was getting from new friends and flings made me feel better about being rejected by my longtime boyfriend, and I'd convinced myself that being skinny was the thing making these new friends and flings possible. If I lost the "progress" I'd made, I wouldn't be wanted or accepted anymore, and I'd have to face the pain of being rejected. That would mean I have to answer the question I didn't want to ask: Am I enough?

I knew I wasn't enough for the guy I thought I was going to marry, so I wanted to at least be enough for myself. I'd prove that I was fine on my own by doing the things that made me happy in the moment. And when the things that made me happy eventually made me miserable, I still assumed I had the power to take back control of my life and get myself on the right path.

It was clear that I didn't. I was actually enslaved by my lifestyle. While my fear of insufficiency fueled my addiction, it also changed me for the worse. Before that last semester of college, I professed and lived Christianity. But after the breakup, I put my faith on the back burner to "focus on my-self." I feared that if I turned to God after the breakup, he would make me sit in my sadness while he healed me. I just didn't have the patience for that. It hurt too much. I wanted quick relief, even if it was fleeting.

I'm grateful for a counselor who pointed me back to God and his Word and told me that not only was what I doing sinful, it was also dangerous. Her four words—"you're going to die"—stopped me in my tracks after a few months of meeting with her.

After that appointment I got into my car, put my head in my hands, and broke down. I cried out to God with a million questions: *How did I get here? And how do I stop? Can I? Can I really let go of this? What will happen if I do? Are you going to be with me? Will you help?*

And he did. After that day the binge-and-purge cycle stopped. While I know this isn't everyone's experience with eating disorders, it was mine. God graciously and immediately gave me the grace to let go of the thing I thought was holding me together. In reality, it was tearing me apart.

I'd been deep in the culture of self-love: doing what I wanted and focusing on my wants in an effort to live my "best life." Ultimately my self-centeredness blinded me to the damage I was wreaking on my life.

I don't know what you're facing now. Whether it's more or less serious than what I faced in college, I can tell you for sure: you're not enough. Just like me, you don't have what it takes to heal yourself: from the addiction, the rejection, or the depression. Your self-contrived solutions to your problems won't work, and your attempts to fill your emptiness with more of yourself will fail. Your insistence upon "doing you" by choosing only what feels good in the moment will only defer the pain until it becomes a crushing burden.

The first step to getting out of whatever unhealthy cycle you're currently in is realizing just how not enough you are. That means letting go of the responsibility to be your own source of fulfillment—a responsibility that was never yours in the first place. AMEN!

THERE'S GOOD NEWS

The world tells us self-love will solve all our problems, but it can't. Lizzo is a popular artist whose calls to self-love characterize her brand. Last year she posted on Instagram a question from one of her followers that read "How is it possible that I listened to the great Lizzo tell me how important self-love is and I still somehow hate myself?" Lizzo responded by saying that self-love takes time, and even she's still not there yet.

But that's not the real reason. Neither Lizzo nor her fan feels content despite focusing on self-love because self-love is inherently unsatisfying. It depends on our feelings, which are subject to constant change based on our circumstances, our performance, and other people's opinions. Self-love is unreliable, conditional, and limited. Chasing after it always brings us to a dead end.

For me, the dead end of self-love looked like a counselor's office hearing that I'm going to die. In my last semester of college, I thought I was doing what freshly single college girls are supposed to do: be "free" and "find myself" by doing exactly what I wanted and when. I looked happy and self-assured, but on the inside, I was rotting. I wanted to find the answer to emptiness inside myself, and it just wasn't there.

I'm not alone in my experience. For a generation obsessed with personal happiness and self-discovery, we're startlingly unhappy and lost. Our rates of depression, anxiety, and suicide are staggering. Even the memes we make highlight the problems that ail us: social anxiety, insomnia, insecurity, a fear of "adulting." At best, we're discontent and confused. At worst, we're totally hollow.

The reason we, a generation living in the most prosperous era in the most prosperous country in the world, still can't find fulfillment is because we're looking for it in the wrong places. We keep hearing that if we just love ourselves a little more and check a few more things off our personal list of goals, we'll finally be okay. This tactic isn't working, and it's keeping us miserable.

Our desperation is exacerbated because of a reason we've

already named: the self can't be both our problem and our solution. If the self is the source of our depression or despair or insecurity or fear, it can't also be the source of our ultimate fulfillment. That means loving ourselves more doesn't satiate us. We need something else—something bigger. Simply, we need Jesus.

There's a reason Jesus describes himself as Living Water and Bread of Life: he satisfies. The searching for peace and for purpose stops in him alone. He created us; therefore only he can tell us who we are and why we're here.

And aren't these the questions everyone's trying to answer: Who are we and why are we here? The world's answer to these questions is "You." *You* define your identity, your purpose, your value, your truth. Jesus's answer is "Me." He defines your identity, your purpose, your value, your truth.

Who do you think is a more reliable source for the answers for which our souls are begging? Jesus—the Maker of the universe—or us—the same people who can barely remember what we had for lunch yesterday?

When we place ourselves on the throne of our lives, giving ourselves the authority to define who we are and why we're here, we inevitably end up where I did in college—exhausted and confused. Why? Because if we're honest with ourselves, we just don't know. We don't know who we're supposed to be, and our ideas of what our purpose is are both changing and elusive. The standards we set for ourselves are ever evolving, so we're never fully content with who we are or what we're doing.

But when Jesus is on the throne of our lives, he has the authority to give us our identity and purpose, and in him, these things never change. In his life he set an example of kindness and love. In his death he paid the debt we owed for our sins so that we could be reconciled to a holy God. In his resurrection he conquered sin and death, so that those who believe can live forever with him.

If we were enough, we wouldn't need Jesus to do these things for us, but we do. Without him we're hopeless, purposeless, and dead in our sin.

When Jesus saves us, we are made new creations and children of God. As such, our goal is to glorify him in everything we do. We don't have to wonder what it's all about anymore. This is it. In exchange for the confusion and exhaustion that comes with trying to be enough, he gives us peace and relief. In exchange for superficial confidence and unsatisfying self-care, Jesus offers us steadfast assurance and trust in his faithfulness.

That's why the fact that you're not enough is not just okay—it's *great*. You aren't meant to be enough, and neither am I.

When we miss this truth, we stay stuck in a vicious cycle of trying to measure up to impossible standards while simultaneously convincing ourselves that we're good enough the way we are. The consequences are always dire.

THE END OF OURSELVES

The tough season I went through in college taught me a lot about the damaging effects of self-love and self-sufficiency, but I'm grateful that it was only a short season. Others have been learning this hard truth their whole lives. I went through a breakup and a subsequent eating disorder. Others have been dealt much harder blows.

Cecily's parents got a divorce a few months before she was born. She and her sister lived with their mom and her boyfriend, Greg.

One of Cecily's first memories is of Greg beating her mother in the bathroom of their apartment. Just four years old, she watched from the hallway as he slammed her mom's head against the tile wall and shoved her limp body to the ground. She remembers thinking she should run and tell someone, but she was scared that if she did, she'd be next.

When the couple wasn't fighting, they were in their own world. They would talk openly about their eagerness for the girls to leave to be with their dad so they wouldn't have to deal with them anymore.

One day Greg left and said he was never coming back. That afternoon Cecily found her mother passed out on the floor by the toilet after overdosing on painkillers. Her sister called their grandmother to tell her their mom was sick. The police arrived within an hour and searched the apartment, discovering dozens of empty pill bottles in the bathroom cabinet. Cecily was only five. The girls were ordered to live full time with their dad, who did his best to raise his girls well. He took them to church, helped them to stay on top of their schoolwork, and encouraged them to be well rounded. He wanted a better life for them than the one he and their mother had led.

Cecily loved her dad and was thankful for the stability he provided. But she still struggled through the aftermath of living with a mom who was unable to love her and her sister. She'd lie awake at night asking *Why doesn't my mom want me? Why am I not enough for her?*

As she grew up, she learned to push these questions away. She lost touch with her mom in her teenage years and moved through life with relative ease, graduating from high school and then from college, building on the firm foundation her dad had worked diligently to lay out for her. When she was twenty-five, she married a man she knew would love her unconditionally. She felt whole for the first time in her life.

Cecily and her husband welcomed two children, a boy and a girl, within three years of their wedding. When she found out she was pregnant the first time, her immediate excitement was quickly replaced by the heavy weight of responsibility to be a better mom for her children than hers had been. Anxious determination consumed her: *This child will never feel the way I did—unwanted, unloved. I'll be everything he wants and needs.*

She quickly learned what a defeating endeavor this was. Their first baby had colic and torticollis, inconsolably crying for five to eight hours a day and sleeping for only an hour at a time at night. But because Cecily insisted upon giving her baby everything she'd never got from her mother, she refused to accept help. She didn't want him to wonder where his mom was when he needed her.

She was worn thin, worry ridden, and depressed. Why couldn't she be all he needed? She couldn't console him, couldn't get him to eat well, and couldn't ease his pain. Every hour of every day was dedicated to being there for him. Why wasn't that enough?

Three months into motherhood, when Cecily finally felt that she had started to get things under control—his colic, her emotions—she found out she was pregnant again. This time, she told herself, she wouldn't be such a mess. She'd learn to master meeting her babies' needs, and she'd finally be confident in her ability to be enough for them.

But it didn't happen that way. Cecily found the demands of caring for a newborn and giving attention to a one-year-old nearly impossible, and she battled guilt because she couldn't give them both all of her attention at the same time. She felt crushed.

She followed Instagram pages and joined Facebook groups dedicated to motivating worn-out moms. She savored the posts that reminded her to take charge of her life and put herself first. They gave her a sense of control she found comforting. Maybe she'd given too much love to her family, and it was time to give some to herself.

So she tried. She shared her struggles online with strangers who told her that she deserved praise and a break.

Mom bloggers and Instagram influencers told her she was discouraged because she was burned out. She was trying too hard. She needed to get rid of the negativity in her life and the toxic people who made her believe that she wasn't enough. She *was* enough, they assured her, and anyone who told her otherwise was wrong. She was not *just* a mom, she was reminded. Who she was before she gave birth was important too, and she needed to love herself more to get that identity back. Motherhood is a defeating, thankless job, they said, and it was important to prioritize other pursuits to make her feel like her "true" self.

She tried her best to apply their advice. She took more time to herself—shopping, working out, getting her nails done, going to dinner with friends. She believed she was beginning to regain her sanity. But she soon found that her renewed feelings of assurance weren't reliable. Some days she would feel competent and confident, and on others she would feel inadequate and alone. Even with the increased time dedicated to self-care, she was still overwhelmed with the responsibility of motherhood. On her dark days she would spill out her feelings to her Facebook friends and scroll through Instagram to gain inspiration, hoping to lighten her burdens. The anxiety would wane, only to return a few hours later. She found that attempting to love herself as she'd been ordered by the self-help gurus actually drained more of her energy than it gave.

After months of trying and failing to effectively manifest these messages of self-empowerment, she'd reached a dead end. One day she stopped to get gas, and when she finished pumping, she realized she'd locked her keys in the car along with

her six-month-old daughter. She erupted in tears, scream-
ing and hitting the windows until a stranger stopped to help
her. Driving home, she realized she was broken.

Cecily thought about killing herself that afternoon. She
didn't know how she'd do it, but she did know that someone
else could take better care of her children than she could.
Surely someone else could be enough for them, even if she
couldn't. She hadn't been enough her whole life—not when
her mom rejected her, and not now. She couldn't deal with it
anymore.

As quickly as the thought of suicide came to her, it left. It
was hard for her even to believe she'd gotten to that point.
That night she confided in her husband, who hugged her and
prayed for her. She slept longer that night than she had in a
while. She woke up the next morning horrified by how low she
had sunk. In obsessing over her happiness, she realized she'd
made herself miserable.

Over the next few weeks Cecily cried out to God for help.
She started to read her Bible again—a part of her morning
routine that she'd replaced with scrolling through social media.
She prayed constantly for God to replace her old self-centered
thoughts with new Christ-centered ones. She trusted Jesus to
carry the burdens she now knew she couldn't bear.

It took reaching her breaking point for Cecily to learn she

would find peace not in *conquering* her not-enoughness, but in embracing it. She realized that God *made her* not enough. She would never have what it took to be everything she and her family needed, and she would never win the affection of her mother. No amount of self-love or affirmation would change that. She needed to go outside of herself for strength, not within. It was by drawing her strength from her Creator that she found peace—even when she couldn't obtain perfection.

Cecily wasn't only attempting to be enough for herself. She was trying to be enough for others. She'd bought into the idea that if she could increase her self-love, she could create a less chaotic life for her family. And yet her family needed more than she could give.

Cecily came to the end of herself, which is the destination for all of us on the road to self-fulfillment and self-love. We're small, frail, and finite, which means we don't have what it takes to love ourselves to wholeness. And we have exactly one comfort: that we serve a God whose reign never ends, whose faithfulness never fails.

Because of that, we are free to empty ourselves rather than build ourselves up with meaningless platitudes about how great and adequate we are. We are led by a Good Shepherd who promises to never let us go thirsty, to ultimately shield us from danger and lead us along a path that is steady and replenishing (Psalm 23). What a relief it is to know it's not up to us to be enough for ourselves or those around us. We have the privilege, as children of God, to "cast all our anxieties on him, because he cares" for us and to allow his power to be perfected in our weakness (1 Peter 5:7).

Whatever your circumstance or struggle, know that you can't make that ache of emptiness go away on your own. No amount of self-care or self-love will get you out of your misery. Even at your most rejuvenated and most lovable, you will still find yourself waking up in the early hours of the morning haunted by the question of what's missing.

You, your plans, and the promises made to you by those peddling self-empowerment will never be enough for you, but Jesus is. In the upcoming chapters, we'll dive into what that God-given purpose looks like as we break down the myths that can prevent us from seeing it.

While the truth that we're just not enough is simple, it's not easy. Unfortunately, young people are bombarded with this lie on a daily basis—and many of us don't even know it.

THE CULT OF SELF-AFFIRMATION

I don't know what your low point looked (or looks) like, but chances are you've been tempted by the superficial comforts of what I've not so affectionately dubbed the Cult of Self-Affirmation—just like Cecily and I were.

The Cult of Self-Affirmation is composed of a ubiquitous network of self-help gurus, self-development experts, and even Christian teachers who pervade social media, line the top charts of Amazon and the shelves of Barnes & Noble, and populate many of our pulpits and even the halls of Congress, all working to affirm the supremacy of the self.

The cult promises peace and salvation if you adhere to its doctrines and assures destruction if you don't. Once you're in, you must abide by its rules. Otherwise, you're out.

In the cult, the god is self, "doing you" is the standard of righteousness, and "following your heart" is the way to salvation. The two key tenets of the cult are Authenticity and Autonomy—being true to yourself and maintaining control over your life. Anyone or anything that attempts to limit who you believe you are is immediately categorized as "toxic" and "judgmental" and is thus pushed to the side.

This is not just a catchy Instagram slogan we're talking

about here. The Cult of Self-Affirmation seeps far deeper than social media into our cultural and political spheres, affecting the moral decisions we make and how we view the world around us. It demands we worship the god of self—a merciless ruler that will stop at nothing to get the service it craves. This is how the god of self demands to be worshipped.

THE HIGH COST OF "DOING YOU"

The cult's clutches extend far beyond mommy culture into the realm of politics and social issues. Its emphasis on autonomy and authenticity as our chief values shows up most apparently in the increasing glorification of abortion.

Shout Your Abortion is an organization that exists to create a space for women to talk about their abortion experiences without guilt or judgment. The hashtag #shoutyourabortion has been used hundreds of thousands of times on Twitter and Instagram by women opening up about their abortions. In 2017, Oprah's website published a post by Shout Your Abortion's founder, lending significant exposure to the viral movement.

The organization anonymously publishes the stories of women who are proud of their choice to end the lives of their preborn children. Theirs is an unapologetic stance, insisting on their website that "abortion is normal." For instance, you won't read accounts from any women who've suffered complications, regretted their decision, or who have since changed their minds about their pro-choice stance and the integrity of Planned Parenthood. Their goal is to remove the so-called stigma surrounding abortion, thus making women feel as comfortable talking about their abortion as they are talking about their trip to the dentist. They embrace authenticity and their unabashed commitment to their bodily autonomy is meant to be seen as liberating. *its not!*

One of the blog posts on the group's website is by a woman named Sarah. Sarah had an abortion when she was twenty-seven. She was in a committed relationship and had a steady job, but she felt that she wasn't ready to have a baby. She writes:

"The abortion wasn't the difficult part. The difficult part was keeping this secret as if it were some deep, dark thing I had to hide. I became anxious and depressed. I went to therapy. I often cried myself to sleep. Not because I thought I made the wrong choice but because other people made me feel I made the wrong choice. . . . And, as it turns out, the average woman who has an abortion is all of us, including me. And now, I live my truth."

In Sarah's story, we see the destructive nature of the Cult

of Self-Affirmation and the hollowness of authenticity and autonomy as supreme values. What happens when we place too much importance on "being yourself" is that we justify choices that hurt us and other people simply because it's "true" to who we are. We convince ourselves that as long as our choice falls in line with who we claim to be, it's good.

This is seen in other cultural conversations of the day as well, such as in the topic of gender and sexuality. Mainstream thought dictates that biology has nothing to do with how we identify, going against basic science and millennia of human history that proves the contrary. But when the god of self rules, none of these facts matter. All that matters is what we want.

This presents serious societal confusion. In 2019, there was a seven-year-old boy named James Younger, who was caught in the middle of a custody battle between his divorced parents. James's mother insisted her son identified as a female and preferred the name "Luna." She planned to encourage James on a path toward puberty blockers and hormone therapy within the next few years. James's dad objected, insisting that he, like his twin brother, identified as a boy and only dressed up as a girl when he was with his mother in an effort to appease her.

The Texas case received little mainstream media coverage but solicited outrage from many parents and commentators on social media, appalled that a mother would subject her son to an irreversible, irrevocably harmful treatment. Whether he believed he was a girl or not was largely irrelevant to those who, like me, were angered by this story. His God-given biology indicates his gender—period. Every compassionate effort, then, should be made to help him reconcile his mind with his body, not the other way around.

The fact that we know so little of the risks associated with pumping cross-sex hormones into a child's still-developing body to block puberty should give us pause enough. The Mayo Clinic reports that such treatment could have damaging effects on a person's fertility. This is a permanent consequence endured by a child, who, statistically, will probably grow out of their gender confusion after puberty.

This is the world ruled by the Cult of Self-Affirmation: one where the only standards of morality are doing what you want to do. So if this little boy *did* insist that he was a girl and wanted to "become" a girl, what justification do his parents or anyone else have to stand in his way? If all that matters is affirming the self, who gets to draw parameters around what's okay and what's not when it comes to someone's—even a child's—identity?

Another example of the dangers of extreme authenticity and autonomy is a recent trend in marriage and relationships called ethical nonmonogamy, which describes the practice of openly and honestly engaging in multiple sexual or nonsexual romantic relationships at once. Here's how Brides.com describes it:

> There is nothing inherently wrong with being in an open, non-monogamous relationship. There is only something wrong if your partner doesn't know you are in an open relationship. You guessed it: Cheating. . . . When a relationship is open, in whatever form that takes for the couple in question, everyone involved knows what is going on. And everyone is happy with the setup. The honesty is the key.

Yikes!

This is the how "morality" within the Cult of Self-Affirmation works: the only standard of right and wrong is how you feel. In the cult, there is nothing inherently good about fidelity or exclusive commitment to a single person. All that matters is that people are happy. This is why, for many people, the Cult of Self-Affirmation is much more appealing than normal religion. It encourages people to do what feels good and removes restrictions and responsibility to others. It values self-love over sacrifice, self-care over service, and self-interest over selflessness. It asks us to give up only that which doesn't please us, and in exchange, it lends us a sense of righteousness.

This is why Christianity and the Cult of Self-Affirmation can't coincide. The values of the Christ follower aren't authenticity and autonomy. They're Christlikeness and obedience. We have an objective standard of right and wrong found in the Bible, which means we're not ruled by cultural trends or our feelings. God's moral standards lead to peace. The cult's lead to chaos and pain.

Authenticity and autonomy certainly aren't bad at all times in all ways, but they *must* be subjected to God's objective standards to produce anything good. Otherwise, they're just trendy-sounding excuses to sin.

Maybe you're thinking the madness caused by the Cult of Self-Affirmation doesn't apply to you. You don't condone the craziness of our current culture, so you feel like you've escaped the cult's clutches. Not so fast. It may be showing up in ways you don't suspect. As important as it is for us to see the cult's effects on the world around us, it's just as important—if not more so—to see how it's manifesting itself right in front of us.

THE CULT'S COMING FOR YOU, TOO

The Cult of Self-Affirmation doesn't offer us a sustainable value system, not as a society or individually. If you're a single woman, the cult's emphasis on authenticity and autonomy will lead you where it led me—to the dead end of "doing me" and control. If you're a mom, the cult's directives to "take back your life" will leave you discontented and bitter. Yup!

Here's what I've learned since having a baby: the cult *loves* to recruit new moms. Its tentacles are all over mommy media: mom blogs, breastfeeding Instagram pages, parenting podcasts—you name it. As a mother of a newborn, you're tired, you're hormonal, you're vulnerable, you're insecure about your postpartum body and worried about your inability to keep your baby alive, which means you're just the right audience for messages of self-affirmation.

Feeling overwhelmed and maybe a bit underappreciated, we moms gravitate toward the insistence of well-meaning momfluencers who tell us what we "deserve"—we "deserve" a break. Praise. Recognition. To take our lives back and to remember that we're more than just a mother. We're told we deserve to be "authentic" selves by reclaiming "autonomy" over our lives and taking back the identity we had before we became moms.

There's some truth in these assurances. We do need a break. It would be nice for our husbands to acknowledge our hard work. We do have roles in addition to being a mom. But the deceptive premise in each of them is that we're *entitled* to a tangible reward for simply doing our job. In that way, motherhood is subtly depicted as something that *happened* to us rather than something we chose and that God graciously gave us.

The Cult of Self-Affirmation wants its members to center their world around them and their feelings. So it makes moms feel like we are *victims* of motherhood rather than what we are: blessed beneficiaries of it. Despite what the cult tells us, Christian moms don't need to build our lives on worldly authenticity and autonomy. Pursuing these things as an escape from the responsibilities of motherhood is the pursuit of the god of self, not the God of Scripture. Motherhood is the calling God has placed on our lives now, and we fulfill that calling for his glory, not for our own recognition.

The cult tells us that the only way to recharge is through self-care and "finding ourselves" outside of our obligation to our families, but that leads nowhere. The only lasting joy we can find in the chaos of parenthood is in the knowledge that even the most mundane, trying moments of motherhood are meant to bring us closer to Christ. When we depend on him for strength in the midst of weakness, for peace in the midst of anxiety, for help in the midst of desperation, when we aim to mimic his unconditional love and self-sacrifice in all that we do for our families, we can rejoice knowing that our effort and exhaustion is never wasted—it's being used for God's glory, for our children's good, and for our sanctification.

Are we not allowed to take time to ourselves then? Of course we are. I'm a new mom and certainly not a parenting expert, but from what I see biblically, there's nothing wrong about trading parenting shifts with our husbands or calling babysitters so we can take naps or get our nails done. God designed us all to need rest. But the *mentality* surrounding our breaks matters.

John Piper tackled a question from a mom on his podcast, *Ask Pastor John*: "Should stay-at-home moms take a day off?" His answer was multifaceted but simple: yes. Moms need rejuvenation. We need a Sabbath. We need help from our husbands, parents, friends, or Sunday school class. Because as much as is expected of us, we're not superhuman. In the episode he reminds us all that it's not selfish to ask the question: "How do you find the pace to finish the race?"

Life is a marathon, not a sprint, which means all of us have to find the rhythms and patterns of activity and rest that allow us to live out the work God has called us to do efficiently and effectively. For me, I've learned that that may mean taking a walk, reading a book, going to bed thirty minutes earlier while my husband puts the baby down, or waking up thirty minutes earlier to make sure I have time to read the Bible before the baby gets up. When our reason behind our rest is to ensure better service to the Lord and to others, we don't have to worry whether or not taking needed breaks is self-centered. It's not.

The Cult of Self-Affirmation encourages us to grab hold of our lives so we don't "lose ourselves" to motherhood. But when we follow Christ, we are never at risk of "losing ourselves," because our identity is eternally found in him. Who we "really are" isn't some mystery we need to solve or path we need to follow. Our sole aim is to honor God by gratefully executing the tasks he's put before us with his help.

What's the connection between the effect the cult has on the world, manifesting itself in the glorification of things like abortion and gender fluidity, and the effect it has on us moms, manifesting itself in everyday selfishness, resentment, and pride?

They're all matters of worship. If we worship the God of Scripture, we trust him. We trust him with unexpected pregnancies. We trust that he made us in the body he meant to make us in. We trust that he has called us and will equip us to be mothers. We trust that his commands are better and more trustworthy than our feelings.

If we worship the god of self, we'll sacrifice anything on its altar to satisfy its demands. And the god of self is *relentlessly* demanding, pushing us even to kill unborn children, damage our bodies, or reject the responsibility of being a mother.

The cult will have us constantly fighting for control and vying for the worship we think we deserve. God asks us to surrender control and to redirect the worship we'd like to give to ourselves to him. This is great news. The yoke of the god of self is difficult and its burden heavy, but God's yoke is easy and his burden light. What a relief to know we don't have to expend our precious energy serving ourselves. We make terrible, unworthy gods.

And because we make unworthy gods, we do one thing really poorly, no matter how hard we try, and that is to come up with our own truth.

The next myth explains why.

MYTH #2

YOU DETERMINE YOUR TRUTH

BACKTEETH BOYS

When I was in second grade, I got my first cavity. The dentist told me he had to put sealants on my teeth to make sure I didn't get another one. I'd never undergone any kind of dental procedure before, so this was a big deal for me. I was nervous. To make me feel better, the hygienist told me that there would be invisible stickers on the sealants—of the Backstreet Boys.

That was all she had to say. I was literally the biggest BSB fan you'd ever met: I had at least three posters in my room, T-shirts, a nightgown, and all of their music. I'd turn off the lights in our family room, listen to their *Millennium* album, and cry—shed actual tears—thinking about the possibility that I might never get to meet them in person. I'd consider very seriously what I would wear to their concert—would I go for something fashionable to show how cute I was or a BSB shirt to prove I was a fan?

I couldn't wait to get my Backstreet Boys sealants on. Even though the hygienist told me they were invisible, I thought that maybe if I looked really hard in the mirror, I'd be able to see them. I never did. But still, I knew they were there, and that was enough.

I am dead serious when I tell you it never, for one second, occurred to me that she was lying. For years—years!—I believed that there was some kind of special technology that enabled dentists to put transparent boy-band stickers on your teeth with your sealants. I'm not even sure when it hit me—maybe high school? It was like I woke up one morning ten years later and realized, *"Oh my gosh. There were never stickers on my teeth!"* I'd been suckered.

I wish I could say that that was the only absurd thing I've believed in my life. In sixth grade I took a picture of Jennifer Aniston circa *Friends* season ten to the hair stylist, convinced that if I just had side bangs, boys would like me. In tenth grade, I thought that my popularity would skyrocket the second I got my braces off.

But the hair stylist in sixth grade told me Jen's haircut would make me look like I had a mullet, so I never got those perfect side bangs. In tenth grade I learned quickly that my coolness and my braces were completely uncorrelated.

Like me, you've been suckered by things that didn't deliver on their promises of fulfillment at some point in your life. Whether it was the Backstreet Boys or S Club 7, side bangs or highlights, drinking or drugs—you've bought into things in your life that ultimately failed to live up to their hype. They were based on a false perception of reality, so they ended up disappointing you or hurting you in the long run.

As we get older, we don't automatically grow out of the tendency to believe things that aren't true; the lies we believe just become more complex and consequential. Our culture encourages us to defer to what's true *for us*, even if it contradicts what *is* true—scientifically, biblically, historically, and so on. This manifests itself in a way we've already discussed—gender ideology, abortion, polyamory, just as examples. But exchanging "my truth" for *the* truth also affects the personal decisions we make and the relationships we build. The results are never good.

YOUR TRUTH WON'T SET YOU FREE

Chloe was a sophomore in college when she was brutally raped by a group of fraternity boys. The friends that came with her to the party had already gone home, and she was left alone, defenseless to their attacks. Traumatized by her experience, she spent the rest of her college career self-medicating with alcohol, sex, and drugs.

Though she managed to graduate on time, Chloe's addiction was out of control. Her parents persuaded her to go to rehab, where she was diagnosed with and treated for PTSD. She was raised a Christian, but she'd pushed God away while she was trying to deal with the pain and shame associated with her rape. At rehab, she started reading her Bible again and committed to following Jesus. She promised herself that she would get clean and stay single for a season while she got her life together.

But as soon as Chloe left rehab, confusion and fear overwhelmed her. What was she going to do with her life? How would she know what direction God wanted her to go in? Would she ever find love?

She felt burdened by the pressure to be and do something worthwhile. Seeing friends on Instagram who were backpacking through Europe, she became inspired by the idea of self-discovery through travel. Even the prospect of exploring the world seemed cathartic. She started following Instagram accounts dedicated to wanderlust that inspired her to embark on her own journey. So two months after coming home from rehab, she pooled the few thousand dollars she had saved and left her family, her friends, and her small hometown in Texas with a one-way ticket to travel the world.

On social media, her life looked like a fairy tale. Her friends and followers praised her from afar for taking what appeared to be brave steps toward inner healing. It seemed to Chloe and to everyone watching that she was living "her truth." Her truth was that she'd been hurt, gone down a dark path of self-destruction, and now was discovering her true self and declaring her worth by setting out on the adventure of her dreams.

But reality looked different. Chloe got involved with a new guy in every town she visited—usually ending up having sex with them. They offered both adventure and security on her winding road of self-discovery. But they all left her high and dry after a few weeks, leaving her feeling used and ashamed.

She was in Paris when she realized her period was late. She took a pregnancy test. It was positive. Then another. Positive again. She couldn't believe it. She was pregnant and totally alone. This time, she had nowhere to run.

Chloe knew she needed to go home. She needed a safe place and support to raise her baby. So she packed her bags and booked the next flight to Texas. She gave birth to her son eight months later.

Now, Chloe loves being a mom, but she regrets the road she took to motherhood. It took becoming unexpectedly pregnant for her to see just how much "her truth" had deceived her. She did everything her friends, favorite authors, motivational speakers, travel bloggers, and Instagram influencers told her she should do to heal her past hurts: embark on a journey to self-discovery, follow her heart, "rumble with her story," indulge her whims, pursue her lust and wanderlust. By giving in and letting go, she thought, she'd finally be happy.

She pursued "her truth" and found that it only led to a dead end. Her travels did nothing to heal the shame and pain she still felt from being raped in college. She did everything she wanted for the months that she explored the world, and yet she left each city feeling more unfulfilled than before. In an effort to "find herself," she got lost.

Chloe's story shows us that we're not enough to come up with our own truths. Our thoughts confuse us. Our intuition is often wrong. Our feelings deceive us. Our desires can be misplaced. And if we put ourselves on the throne of our own lives, deeming ourselves our own arbiter of truth, our heart, thoughts, intuition, feelings, and desires are all we have to lead us. We're stuck looking to ourselves for insight that just isn't there. On our own, we don't know where we're going. To reiterate: we'd make terrible gods.

Bestselling author and motivational speaker Brené Brown writes in her book *Braving the Wilderness*: "The truth about who we are lives in our hearts."

This mentality explains the "why" behind the persistence of so many people to constantly follow their hearts and pursue constant introspection. They're looking for the truth they've been told by the world of self-healing and self-love that is buried there, deep within.

Through various catharses—traveling, new relationships, meditation, therapy—we search for this truth that will finally reveal to us our identity and worth. We try the *Eat, Pray, Love*–type method and hope that our adventures, whimsy, and self-evaluation will help us uncover past trauma or confront old mistakes.

We take a journey much like Chloe's—searching the world for her deep and hidden "truth" somewhere within. But what we find is that even when we've followed our hearts and wrestled with our pasts, we're still hungry for more. We still don't feel healed or complete.

I found this out for myself. I pursued "my truth" during that season in college when I was addicted to drinking, hooking up, and bingeing/purging. In an effort to feel better about myself in the face of heartbreak and rejection, I tried to build a new life based on a new value system. That value system was composed entirely of what made me feel good in the moment.

I was tired of being sad, of wallowing in self-pity, and fretting over my future, so the instant gratification that comes with getting drunk and the ego boost from superficial flings were attractive to me. I'd lost a relationship that hadn't just defined who I was then, but also who I thought I'd be in the future. I'd been the girl in a serious relationship who was going to get married right after college, and then suddenly I wasn't. As my plans crumbled, I struggled to know who I was.

It didn't help that I had shingles the night he broke up with me. You know shingles as the rash your grandmother and her nursing home friends had last winter. I had it at twenty-one. Shingles produces a rash that forms clusters of red, painful, itchy blisters and usually shows up on your back or side. Not for me! Mine stretched across my neck and face. It was terrible. It was ugly and painful. Needless to say, when my boyfriend showed up to "talk" one night, I looked and felt like a miserable mess.

As uncomfortable as it is to admit, I think part of my motivation for my weight loss was wanting to somehow make up for how unattractive and unwanted I felt in that moment. I thought that if I was skinnier, I'd be more lovable. The attention I got from guys as a freshly single girl affirmed that mentality. The alcohol was just a numbing agent so I wouldn't have to deal with it all. Similar to Chloe, I didn't want to admit what was really going on, so I masked it.

"My truth" during this season was that I deserved to feel good about myself. I'd spent nearly three years prioritizing a boyfriend, and now it was time to focus on me. I was entitled to have fun and let loose, and I was even convinced that doing so might be healing for me. I could be free from the expectations he had for me that I couldn't meet and just be myself— *authentic*. If I wasn't enough for him, I told myself, that's fine. I can be enough for myself. And I'll prove it by doing exactly what I wanted, when I wanted.

If you'd been an outside observer of this version of college Allie, you might have thought I was living my best life. I was working out, making new friends, going on dates, and attending parties on the weekends. I was still managing to do well in my classes, and I was even chosen to deliver the student speech at our graduation ceremony. You might have thought I'd come into my own, as if I'd finally found myself. You probably would have assumed I'd gotten over my heartache and moved on.

But I was broken. Almost every time I drank too much, I became a crying mess. Once I let my guard down, it was obvious I wasn't okay. My sadness over the breakup was compounded by the guilt I felt for drinking too much or hooking up with another guy. Before that semester, people knew me as a girl who led Bible studies and served as chaplain for our sorority. I'd let that go in favor of "doing me." In other words, I was worshipping the god of self.

We know where that got me—to a counselor's office hearing my eating disorder was going to be fatal if I didn't stop. Because I wanted to be enough on my own, I'd replaced God and his truth as the center of my universe with myself, proclaiming my own sovereignty over right and wrong, good and bad. Without realizing it, I was a card-carrying member of the Cult of Self-Affirmation, prioritizing my authenticity and autonomy above all else.

What I learned the hard way was that if I really wanted a path that leads to peace, I needed a standard outside myself to tell me what's true and good. That standard is God.

In *Mere Christianity,* C. S. Lewis argues for the existence of a universal moral law that all human beings, regardless of culture, inherently aim to follow. Without it, we have no right to feel outrage toward horrors like slavery or the Holocaust. But we do. That's because there is a sense of morality embedded in each of us, given to us by a Moral Lawgiver. Without a Moral Lawgiver, there is no moral law. With no transcendent moral law or lawgiver, we are all our own gods, and no one can say who's right and who's wrong. This puts our lives into a tailspin of chaos.

I was a beneficiary of this chaos—and I didn't have to be. When we first broke up, I was afraid to go to God with my sadness, because I knew he probably wouldn't give me a quick fix. Being obedient to him would mean not getting drunk, not hooking up with guys, and not hurting my body with unhealthy eating habits, which were all methods to numb my pain. Letting these things go and instead turning to the Lord would mean I actually had to feel the hurt, and I didn't want to do that.

But what I realized months later is that the pain I would have felt if I'd walked with God in those first aching days would have been far better than the pain and shame and regret I felt after months of going my own way. Time spent worshipping the God of Scripture is never time wasted, but time spent worshipping the god of self is.

I didn't start healing from heartache until I stopped submitting to my own standards for right and wrong, which were based on what felt good, and submitted to God's standards for right and wrong, which are based on what *is* good. God's truth is what we use to determine what's true and what's not, not ourselves. Because while our feelings change and mislead us, God's Word never will.

Here's what we need to recognize: "our truth" is usually Satan's lie. What feels true to us in the moment may not be true, good, or trustworthy at all. While it's *true* that we have experiences and trauma that shape us, these things don't equate to moral *truths*. They just happened. And maybe they were significant, and maybe they taught us something. But in order to know whether these lessons we learned are truths worth building our lives on, we have to compare them to *the* standard of truth, God's Word.

We are not enough to decide the truth, but God is. This is good news! Because the me who once believed the Backstreet Boys were plastered on my molars, the me who has chased after all kinds of damaging myths and lies in an effort to find fulfillment, isn't equipped now to be the determinant of truth. And you aren't either. It's a burden none of us is strong enough to bear, and we don't have to.

But in order to replace our truth with God's truth, we first have to know what it is.

MEOLOGY

Thankfully, as Christians, we don't have to guess at God's definitions of right and wrong. He tells us in the Bible, which is inerrant, infallible, and sufficient for instruction.

I grew up going to church and attended a Christian school. When I was little, everyone I knew who was my age had the same Bible: the NIV *New Adventure Bible*. It was awesome. Real-life application, historical tidbits, memory verse suggestions, a pink and purple cover. I found my copy in my old closet the other day, and I opened it to find most pages completely soaked in pink and green highlighter, the margins filled with drawings of cats, some menorah sketches in the book of Numbers, and lots of random segments cut out for who knows what reason.

As little as my seven-year-old self understood the Bible, I'm grateful for the time my teachers and parents took in helping us learn it. Studying God's Word is necessary for Christians to form their worldviews and establish their moral compasses, and yet, tragically, many Americans who identify as Christians don't know their Bibles. They consequently hold to a faith that's a mixture of God's truth and their own truth.

Every two years Ligonier Ministries conducts a survey to gauge American evangelical Christians' theological understanding. The 2018 study reveals deep misunderstandings among self-identified evangelicals about the person of Jesus, sin, and salvation.

Perhaps the most troubling part of the study was the respondents' perception of truth. Thirty-two percent of respondents agreed with this statement: "Religious belief is a matter of personal opinion; it is not about objective truth." Additionally, 51 percent agree that God accepts the worship of all religions, not just Christianity. This means a large portion of Christians in the United States claim a set of beliefs that they're not confident is true.

The good news is that for many Christians, the intentions are good. They want to study the Bible, but they don't know how. The Bible can be overwhelming, complex, and confusing. So instead of reading it closely, many Christians opt to read devotionals or listen to sermons that they feel are easier to understand and are more applicable to their lives.

The problem is that many devotionals are oversimplified, and even the best sermons don't offer the wisdom the Bible does. Furthermore, many popular devotional authors and preachers today simply don't teach the Bible. Instead, they preach what I call meology—or me-centered theology. Rather than teaching what Scripture means and what it says about God, they highlight what Scripture means *to us* and what it says about us. Meology seeks to comfort at the expense of conviction. This results in readers who are both misinformed and uninformed about the nature of God. The consequence is people who are unsure of the truth he offers.

Two of the most popular forms of meology today are found in the prosperity gospel and in what I call hipster Jesus Christianity. Prosperity teachers like Joel Osteen, Paula White,

Kenneth Copeland, and others preach messages that guarantee God's material and monetary gifts in exchange for faith. Osteen describes his job as "helping people sleep at night," rather than making people feel "ashamed." Paula White, spiritual adviser to President Trump, declared on TBN in 2007 that "anyone who tells you to deny yourself is from Satan" (Jesus said that). Kenneth Copeland preaches that Jesus "won financial prosperity" on the cross. In the name of comfort and hope, health-and-wealth preachers offer a powerless gospel. While this doctrine scratches "itching ears," it doesn't save (2 Timothy 4:3), because it's not true. While God may choose to bless us with health and wealth for his glory, he doesn't guarantee them. Instead, he assures us that we will suffer for his sake. He promises persecution, not promotions (Matthew 10:16).

The prosperity gospel exchanges God's truth of promised hardship for our "truth" of entitlement to an easy life or overflowing bank account. It views God as a genie aroused by "naming it and claiming it." But Job 1:21 tells us that God both gives and takes, and that either way, his name is to be praised. Our "truth" is that we want God's stuff. *The* truth is that God has given us something better than stuff—himself.

If we view Scripture through the lens of the prosperity gospel, we see the biblical narrative centered on us and what

God can do for us, rather than on God, what he's done for us through Christ, and how we can serve him. This is the danger of meology: it misses the truth. And when we miss the truth of Christianity we lose everything: salvation, joy, sanctification, intimacy with God. Our very souls are at stake when we exchange God's truth for ours.

On the other side of the meology coin is Hipster Jesus Christianity. Hipster Jesus is a go-with-the-flow kind of guy whose highest priority is our happiness. He's not big on institutionalized religion, doesn't care about sin, and just wants us to feel good about ourselves. According to Hipster Jesus, the only wrong is saying that there's wrong.

Glennon Doyle, known for her popular blog *Momastery*, represents Hipster Jesus Christianity. She wrote the 2017 bestselling book *Love Warrior*, about fighting for her marriage, with her husband. Her life changed when she met U.S. Women's National Soccer Team player Abby Wambach, with whom she quickly fell in love. Doyle later left her husband and married Wambach.

Now Doyle encourages women to follow her brand of authenticity. When asked how, as a Christian, she justifies her divorce and remarriage to a woman, she said, "I don't spend my precious time and energy justifying myself to anybody. That sounds exhausting. The most revolutionary thing a woman can do is not explain herself!" She claims that the Bible is indifferent toward same-sex marriage and monogamy, and that to think it did teach about these practices would be to "rub up against what I know about the God of love."

Josh Harris, who was a significant figure in evangelicalism in the 1990s and 2000s, was also lured by the Hipster Jesus trend. He wrote a book about courtship called *I Kissed Dating Goodbye* in 1997 that became central to purity culture within the church. Harris pastored a church in Maryland while raising his children alongside his wife. In 2019, he announced that he and his wife would be getting a divorce. Days later he shared a post announcing that he is no longer a Christian and issued an apology to the LGBTQ community for "standing against marriage equality" and for not "affirming [them] and [their] place in the church."

Of course the Bible is clear on the issue of sexuality. The definition of marriage as between a man and a woman is rooted in creation and reiterated in the New Testament as representative of Christ and the church and is therefore reflective of the Gospel. It's not just based on a couple of verses some people have deemed irrelevant. God's definition of marriage has both physical and spiritual significance—*Gospel* significance.

This reality is missable only if we insist upon putting our truth over *the* truth. This is the core problem with the theology of Hipster Jesus Christianity—not that its proponents often deny biblical authority on sexuality, but that it denies biblical authority *period*. This so often leads to a denunciation of Christianity altogether in exchange for a form of agnosticism. It's impossible to simultaneously submit to the God of Scripture and the god of self.

Neither the prosperity gospel nor Hipster Jesus Christianity have much to say about sin, because meology—like the Cult of Self-Affirmation—is concerned with temporary happiness rather than lasting holiness. Meology of any kind looks nothing like Jesus's teachings.

The one, true Jesus cares so much about our sin that he endured a gruesome death on a cross to save us from it. On earth he healed and he comforted, but he also called those he encountered to repentance (Matthew 4:17).

Jesus defined sin as not just what we do outwardly, but also as what we think and feel on the inside. He said it's not enough that we don't commit adultery; we also shouldn't lust. He said it's not enough not to kill someone; we shouldn't even hate them. Jesus raised the standard of goodness to another level, insisting that we love our enemies and pray for those who persecute us rather than retaliate. It's a righteousness only possible through him.

The prosperity gospel and Hipster Jesus Christianity are self-worship disguised as genuine faith. They focus on what we think we deserve rather than who God is. They obscure the true Gospel in exchange for a message that appeals to our natural self-centeredness. As John Piper says of the prosperity gospel, they are doctrines that "clothe the eternal gospel of Christ in the garments of worldliness."

Meology leads not only to the theological confusion we see reflected in the Ligonier study, but also to faithlessness.

Our aim in studying the Bible is to know God. In learning his character and his truth, our view of ourselves and of the world are consequently shaped. Scripture provides a firm, unchangeable foundation for our lives that secular self-help and "Christian" meology don't and can't.

That means reading our Bibles is crucial in differentiating between our truth, which leads to confusion, and *the* truth, which leads to life, joy, and peace.

But the question stands: *How* do we read the Bible? There are lots of good resources on this, but I'll give you my advice: get a good study Bible. I love the ESV Study Bible. Start in the book of John. You can read it fast or slow, by chapter or verse by verse. Try to answer these questions when you read (see box):

Praying for wisdom from the Holy Spirit, Christians use these questions to dig into what Scripture actually means, not just what it means *to us*:

What's the historical context of this passage?
How does this fit with Scripture as a whole?
Why was this written?
Who was the audience?
What does this verse tell me about God?
Is there a sin I should repent or an action I need to take?

You're not going to understand everything. I don't. That's okay. Pray for wisdom—something God promises to give to those who ask (James 1:5). Trust that you are going to the sole source of truth.

Jesus said that he is "*the* way, and *the* truth, and *the* life" and that "*no one* comes to the Father except through" him (John 14:6). John 1:14 describes Jesus as "full of grace and truth." Jesus tells us in John 8:30–32, "If you abide in my word, you are truly my disciples, and you will know the truth, and the truth will set you free." Jesus asks God the Father in John 17:17 to "sanctify" his people "in truth," because "your word is truth." How awesome to know the source of truth isn't somewhere "out there" or buried deep within us. It's in Jesus, who has made himself available to us.

If you're feeling overwhelmed by the prospect of studying Scripture, that's okay. The good news is that you don't have to pursue truth alone.

TAKE ME TO CHURCH

My husband and I spent way too long in the first few years of our marriage church shopping, looking for the place that met all our qualifications: dynamic pastor, lots of young people in our life stage, good small-group structure, and trendy-but-not-too-trendy worship leaders. Eventually, though, we got tired of the search. We started slipping into the habit of listening to a sermon podcast or watching a service online on Sundays rather than going through the trouble of trying out a new church.

But we were both convicted by the fact we both knew: this is not what church is about. It's not about us or what we get from it. Churches are to exist in local communities to encourage and instruct Christians in God's Word, to meet the needs of fellow believers, and to equip members to share the Gospel and serve their neighbors and the "least of these." The hours we spend in church should be defined by self-forgetfulness, not self-fulfillment.

That doesn't mean we shouldn't enjoy our pastor's sermons or the style of worship, but it does mean there may never be a church that checks all of your boxes. There may be many characteristics that make a good church, but the most important one is this: the Gospel—the biblical truth about sin, salvation through Jesus, and sanctification—is preached.

Why does this take precedence over what kinds of missions the church is a part of or how well run the children's ministry is? Because without the Gospel as the driving force of all a church does, mission trips are just Instagram opportunities, and the children's ministry is just glorified day care. The Gospel is the core reason churches exist, and it's to define all that we as Christians do.

A pastor who preaches the Gospel will be one who bases his sermons not on his opinion, but on the Word of God. A pastor can only preach correctly about sin, sanctification, and salvation by basing his teaching on the Bible. His sermons will be steeped in the wisdom of the Bible. They won't sound like a motivational speaker or a self-help guru. They might be entertaining and dynamic, but no matter the charisma of the preacher, the message will be centered on God's Word.

A good question to ask when listening to preachers is: Is he providing context and pointing us to *Christ*, or is he extracting verses to fit a predetermined message and pointing us to ourselves?

For example, a pastor who teaches the story of David and Goliath as a metaphor for Christians slaying their giants isn't pointing his congregants to God. We are *not* David in this story—Jesus is. *He* slayed the ultimate giant—sin and death—when he died on the cross for our transgressions and rose again three days later. As Sinclair Ferguson states in his book, *Preaching the Gospel from the New Testament*: "Jesus is the true and better David, whose victory becomes his people's victory, though they never lifted a stone to accomplish it themselves."

And how much better a message is that—that we're not our own heroes, but God is? This is the privilege of being a Christian: shaking off the pressure of being our own gods and instead relying on the Savior, who is steadfast and sure.

Biblical theology gives us solid ground where meology offers sinking sand. Any pastor whose sermons glorify and coddle his congregants rather than point them to God, his glory, and his Gospel is doing an eternal disservice to his congregants, and it's not a church we need to be a part of. A healthy, thriving church will base all they say and do on Scripture, and the good news of Jesus's death and resurrection will be at the center of their sermons, ministries, and local and global mission work.

Many churches' exchange of biblically sound preaching for motivational talks with Bible verses sprinkled in is a huge reason why, as the Ligonier study cited, so many self-identified Christians are theologically confused, exchanging real truth for personal truth. If we're not taught God's character and will from the shepherds of our churches, we'll turn to social media, to influencers both spiritual and secular, to politicians, to our friends, and to ourselves to help us shape our worldviews. This leaves us with a contradictory and unstable meology that will inevitably lead to living a life contradictory to the one God has called us to live: holy, joyful, helpful, and truthful.

Isn't it a relief to know we don't have to see every country, kiss every guy, and take every turn on the road of self-discovery to find truth? It's available to us in God himself, whose wisdom Christians have access to through Christ. Our truth is both elusive and unsatisfying. God's truth is present and sustaining. While the world tells us our truths are somehow simultaneously within us and "out there," God gives us real truth in himself here and now.

As available as God's truth is, though, understanding it is a lifelong process.

A TRAJECTORY TOWARD TRUTH

Thankfully, God gives us grace for the journey. When I first became a Christian, I consumed all kinds of sermons and books that weren't biblically sound. While I read C. S. Lewis, I also read books by Rob Bell, who has since come out as a Universalist, believing all people are ultimately destined for heaven. I listened to Joel Osteen regularly, not recognizing that his promise of health and wealth is unbiblical. I had a form of meology that was reflective of a girl who didn't know her Bible. Only through God's patience, study, and time have I learned how to let the Bible inform my theology. And I've got a long way to go yet.

The Holy Spirit guides us, convicts us, molds us, and moves us—though usually not all at once. A person led by Christ should be on a trajectory toward truth, which means we don't know everything now that we'll know in a year. There will be sins we're unaware of today that we may be repenting next week. There is selfishness we're clinging to today that we will be asked to relinquish tomorrow.

Throughout our lives, through the power of the Holy Spirit, wisdom of God's Word, and the equipping of the church, we are to work "to reach the stature of the fullness of Christ," becoming more like him in every season (Ephesians 4:13).

This doesn't mean our path will be a straight line from A to B, but it does mean our lives should mean our path is paved by truth—*God's* truth, not ours.

Our adherence to God's truth doesn't just influence how we read the Bible or what churches we choose; it also affects how we decide right and wrong in general.

In exploring this, we're about to wade into some deeper (and more controversial) waters. Track with me as we dive into how the "my truth" mentality has infected culture and politics.

CANCELED

Following God means embracing a love not for our own truth but for objective truth. We look to the Bible as the steady standard of right and wrong. Without a belief in God as the final moral authority, people are left to their own devices to determine good versus bad. And if, as the Cult of Self-Affirmation dictates, we are all our own gods, who's to say whose moral code is enforceable? As you can tell, this kind of moral subjectivism sounds like confusion and chaos. That's because it is. Cue: cancel culture.

In February 2019, eighteen-time Grand Slam tennis champion Martina Navratilova wrote a piece for *The Sunday Times* that landed her in what she later described as a "hornets' nest" of controversy.

In the article she argued that it was "cheating" that "hundreds of athletes who have changed gender by declaration and limited hormone treatment have already achieved honors as women that were beyond their capabilities as men." The transactivist group Trans Actual labeled these comments "transphobic" and tweeted their disagreement with the article. Navratilova, a lesbian, was then quickly dropped by Athlete Ally, a group that advocates for LGBTQ athletes and that had previously supported her. The Twitter outrage mob condemned her as a hateful bigot.

Of course, by any logical standard, Navratilova is right. What we learned in sixth grade biology hasn't changed, even if cultural standards have. Men have greater bone density than women, higher aerobic and anaerobic capacity, more muscle mass, and are, in general, more aggressive than women, even when hormone treatments that decrease testosterone slightly diminish these characteristics. This gives most men who identify as women an advantage over biological women in athletic competitions.

This is proven by the International Olympic Committee's own standards for transathletes. Though women who identify as men can engage in men's competitions without restriction, men who declare themselves women must prove that their testosterone levels have been below a certain point for twelve months before competing. If there were no significant physical differences between men and women, no rules regarding transathletes would be necessary. But there are. The rule is an attempt to minimize a biological gap between men and women that can never be fully closed.

Navratilova knows the athletic advantage men have first-hand. In 1992, she played Jimmy Connors in a pay-per-view show in Las Vegas. Connors was allowed only one serve, and Navratilova could hit into the doubles alleys. Still, Connors won 7–5, 6–2. In 1998, German tennis player Karsten Braasch (ranked 203 in the world) played a match against each Williams sister and won soundly against both. Serena Williams herself remarked in 2013 that if she were up against a player like Andy Murray, she'd "lose 6–0, 6–0, in five to six minutes."

None of these factors are considered, however, in the realm of Cancel Culture. "Canceled" is what happens to you when the court of public opinion (held primarily on Twitter) decides that something you've said or done at any time in your life is unacceptable by today's social and moral standards. Cancelers call for boycotts of your shows or products, demand that you be fired from your place of employment, command that you be deplatformed from social media and the apps that host your content, target your advertisers, and pressure organizations associated with you to disavow you. They take no prisoners.

Cancel Culture is the perfect depiction of how the secular world does morality without absolute truth: the boundaries of righteousness are ever changing based on the latest social whim. Because there's no objective standard of right and wrong, people's feelings are all we can base morality on. That means the group with the most cultural sway is typically in charge. What was acceptable yesterday, then, won't be acceptable tomorrow, and so on.

Sometimes people are canceled for the right reasons. Consider Harvey Weinstein, the Hollywood producer and accused serial sexual assaulter. In 2017, journalists at *The New York Times* uncovered three decades of substantial allegations of sexual misconduct that included offering movie roles to actresses in exchange for sex. Ronan Farrow reported for *The New Yorker* that thirteen women had accused Weinstein of sexual assault or harassment, and three women accused him of rape. Since these allegations surfaced, more than eighty women have claimed to be victims of Weinstein's predation.

The outcry against Weinstein was immediate and catalytic. The scandal catapulted the celebrity-led #MeToo and Time's Up movements, which focused mostly on women sharing stories of harassment or assault. Since 2017, a number of prominent figures have stepped forward and revealed their experiences with sexual abuse. The rage against Weinstein and others like him is still the center of many cultural conversations about power and consent.

But there's still a problem with all of this. While Weinstein certainly deserves his cancellation, he didn't *suddenly* become a known predator. His reputation as a creep was an open secret in Hollywood long before the reports came out. Some celebrities—Gwyneth Paltrow, Courtney Love, and Seth MacFarlane—alluded to Weinstein's behavior publicly more than a decade earlier. In December 2017, *The New York Times* published a piece titled "Weinstein's Complicity Machine," which analyzed Weinstein's "wall of invulnerability" built by powerful Hollywood elites and via his support of Democratic politicians, such as the Clintons and the Obamas.

For probably the first time ever, celebrities were speaking out about sexual ethics. The behaviors they suddenly found the courage to condemn have long been condemned by people outside of Hollywood. Suddenly it became trendy to care about sexual behavior and power dynamics. But those of us with a biblical worldview didn't need Hollywood to tell us what we've always known: actions like those of Harvey Weinstein are wrong.

I think a lot of good has come from the Me Too movement. Women previously too scared to come forward with their stories found the strength to speak up. Predators in Hollywood and in major media corporations have been held to account. But it's also shown us the volatility of morality based primarily on outrage. Its standards are fickle and unreliable. It's swayed by "my truths," which change, rather than the truth, which doesn't.

In 2018, Dr. Christine Blasey Ford brought a serious allegation of sexual assault against Supreme Court nominee Brett Kavanaugh—that he had forced himself on her and presumably attempted to rape her at a party when they were seventeen. Ultimately the claims remained unverifiable, and Kavanaugh was confirmed.

The feminist mantra of the Kavanaugh saga was: "believe all women." Not listen to all women. Not pay attention to their stories. Not take them seriously. But *believe* them. The standard shifted from hearing women's accounts to fully accepting them without question, as the outrage toward toxic masculinity, coupled with a fear of a conservative justice, dictated. No matter where you stood on the Kavanaugh debacle, it's easy to see that that kind of mentality isn't based on truth, but on cultural trends, political expediency, and emotion. That's not a just standard for anyone.

Without objective benchmarks for right and wrong, this is

about the best a world ruled by subjective truth can do: accept morality defined by the mob. Whoever controls our means of communication and information arbitrates what's true and what's false, what's right and what's wrong, and who's canceled and who's not.

This is not a culture Christians should be a part of. We don't discern good and evil based on the latest rage trend. We don't use Twitter as our source of truth; we use God's Word, which never changes. We don't have to be tossed by the waves of cultural relevance. We have God's absolute truth as our anchor.

This doesn't mean Christians don't get it wrong. There were Christians who attempted to justify slavery by using the Bible. There are people today who may try to condone the abuse of women via the biblical command for wives to submit to their husbands. But these sinful misinterpretations speak not to God's infallibility but ours.

No matter what the mainstream once believed, even those who identified as Christians, slavery was always wrong. It was always the objectification and degradation of people made in God's image. Any kind of abuse, extortion, or injustice is and has always been wrong because God says so, not because celebrities or politicians or courts or influencers say so.

William Wilberforce, who led the way for the abolition of

slavery in England, said it best: "What a difference it would be if our system of morality were based on the Bible instead of the standards devised by cultural Christians." I would add, "or by culture, period."

There is freedom in realizing that neither we nor anyone else has authority to determine truth and morality. "My truth" and society's "truth" are ever changing, arbitrary, and exhausting to keep up with. Sometimes outrage is justified, but that justification is not defined by people in power; it is defined by God.

Resisting the world's fluctuating morality isn't easy, especially when the "cause" sounds good—even biblical.

SOCIAL JUSTICE

You've probably heard the term "social justice." A concept originally used by the Catholic Church to describe the kind of service and policies that benefited the poor and the marginalized, social justice has evolved to be inclusive of mostly left-leaning policies such as the redistribution of wealth, abortion, socialized health care, and unrestrictive immigration policies.

Social justice has become both a list of causes to care about and a way to view the world. It's the modern determinant of virtue, and yet its foundation is subjective "truths," not abso-

NOT THROUGH BIBLICAL WORLD VIEW; BUT THROUGH LENS OF critical theory, critical race theory, queer theory

lute truth. Because of that, though it sounds compassionate and courageous, it's not a sphere we need to be in.

"Social justice warrior" has become a pejorative for the perpetually offended, but the social justice worldview is more complex (and more significant) than political correctness and hypersensitivity. It serves as the lens through which today's mainstream political and social spheres see the world.

The goal with which social justice is primarily concerned is equality. Where there is disparity—in wealth, in prison sentencing, in graduation rates, in success, in representation, in treatment, and so on—social justice advocates see injustice. Categorizing people as either "oppressed" or "oppressors," defenders of social justice aim to push down the oppressor and uplift the oppressed, closing the gap between the two groups.

Social justice uses intersectionality to determine who qualifies as the oppressed and who qualifies as the oppressor. Intersectionality takes stock of an individual's characteristics, such as race, nationality, or sexual orientation, and assigns them oppression "points," for lack of a better term, based on how many historically marginalized identity groups they belong to. The more points you have, the more likely you are to be considered on the side of the oppressed.

For example, in the world of intersectionality-fueled social justice, a man is viewed as more privileged than a woman, so the man takes on the role of the oppressor, and the woman, the oppressed. To see how this plays out in real life, consider the issue of the "gender wage gap."

The claim is that women make $0.79 for every $1.00 a man makes, which points to patriarchal oppression of women. The solution proposed is another federal law, in addition to the Equal Pay Act already passed in 1963, that will ensure equal pay between men and women.

The claim is true—in a sense. Women do make $0.79 to every $1.00 a man makes when factors such as hours worked, education earned, or positions held are not considered. This is called the uncontrolled gap. But when all factors are the same, women make more than $0.99 to every $1.00 a man makes—a difference that's within the margin of error. In other words, the "wage gap" between men and women is virtually non-existent, and even if a slight gap exists, there is little proof that injustice is to blame.

Sweden, one of the most egalitarian and progressive countries in the world, has taken every legislative effort to shrink the gap between the earnings of men and women, such as guaranteeing equal parental paid leave. And yet women in Sweden still make significantly less than men make.

Why? Because of the choices women make. They still account for the vast majority of parental leave taken in the workforce. They work fewer hours on average than men. They tend to choose career paths that are less lucrative than most men's. Women and men, even in a society ruled by social justice, are still inherently different and therefore the outcomes of each group will not be the same.

The assumption that differences always imply discrimination is based on feeling rather than fact. In his book *The Quest for Cosmic Justice,* economist Thomas Sowell exchanges the term "social justice" for "cosmic justice" because of the unreachable, intangible results social justice advocates fight for. Sowell describes cosmic justice this way:

> Cosmic justice . . . is about putting particular segments of society in the position that they would have been in but for some undeserved misfortune. This conception of fairness requires that third parties must wield the power to control outcomes, over-riding rules [or] standards.

Social justice is concerned not with equality of opportunity but equality of outcomes. In order to achieve this, it must hold back those who are ahead and push forward those who are behind. Equality of outcome is *never* possible without government force.

Examples of social justice are racial reparations, which redistribute the wealth of white people in the United States to black people to compensate for the decades-long effects of slavery; affirmative action, which gives preferential treatment to students of certain races over others; or socialism, which takes money from those at the top and gives it to those at the bottom in an effort to achieve wealth equality. All of these effectively punish the more "privileged" groups in favor of the groups considered less privileged.

Of course some gaps do point to real injustice. Obviously, in the Jim Crow South, the inequality between white and black people was due to horrific discrimination and racism. The Supreme Court's ruling that "separate but equal" was inherently unequal was a righteous one.

The difference is that, this ruling was based on *provable* injustice, not on *perceived* injustice. This is the key difference between social justice and actual justice. The former deals in perception; the latter deals in proof. And this is why Christians should care: we follow God, the transcendent Lawgiver, which means we are indebted to the truth in all things.

If God is our only source of morality and truth, that means he also defines justice. And according to the Bible, God's justice doesn't judge people based on their identity groups. Biblical justice is concerned with righteousness, not with an arbitrary calculation of how to hold back one group and lift another to achieve equal outcomes.

Leviticus 19:15 explains God's idea of righteous justice: "You shall do no injustice in court. You shall not be partial to the poor nor defer to the great, but in righteousness shall you judge your neighbor."

God opposes partiality either to the weak or to the strong. As James 2:8–9 says, "If you really fulfill the royal law according to the Scripture, 'You shall love your neighbor as yourself,' you are doing well. But if you show partiality, you are committing sin and are convicted by the law as transgressors."

God is a god of justice. He cares about it—not just in a court of law but in how we treat the truly marginalized: the outcast, the poor, the vulnerable, and the victim. God's justice means restoration for the downtrodden as much as it means repercussions for the wrongdoer.

That means Christians indeed care about a range of justice-related issues, including racism, misogyny, extorting the poor, abuse, and sex trafficking, to name a few. We work to replace hate with peace and injustice with justice. We believe in holding those who do wrong to account and fighting for the innocent.

But our fight for the "least of these" needn't be lumped in

with the secular world's definition of "social justice." Biblical justice is both truthful and direct; it does not advocate for punishing entire groups based on perceptions of privilege. It does not demand that those whom one group views as more privileged hand over their earnings to the government to be redistributed as the government sees fit. When Jesus calls his followers to care for the "least of these," that is an individual mandate, not a bureaucratic one (Matthew 25:40).

Christians are not commanded to seek equal outcomes based on perceived group oppression, because, first, we know that such outcomes are impossible. As Thomas Sowell points out, "If two people from the same family, raised in the same home, have different outcomes in their lives, how can we expect people from different backgrounds to have the same outcome?"

Second, Christians don't view people through the lens of their collective grievances. We view people as individuals, made in the image of God, valuable and equal, all dead in sin apart from Christ and responsible for his or her actions. The Bible doesn't give us any other option for how to view one another. Our experiences and even ethnicities matter, but they don't ultimately define us. We are defined by Jesus. There is no place for intersectionality in the body of Christ.

This doesn't discount the disadvantages people indeed face nor the uneven playing field that inevitably characterizes life on earth, and it certainly doesn't abdicate our responsibility as Christians to help those in need. The Bible is clear: "to whom much is given, much is required" (Luke 12:48). And "'Truly, I say to you, as you did it to one of the least of these my brothers, you did it to me'" (Matthew 25:40).

But Christians need to understand that this isn't the job of the government, and this isn't "social justice." This is the work of the church. This is what Christians have always been called to do. And it is not fueled by resentment for those who have more than we do but by the power of the Gospel, which calls us to love others indiscriminately—literally "as yourself" (Galatians 5:14). This Gospel has been the sufficient driver of true justice as long as it's existed.

It is this Gospel that compelled William Wilberforce to lead the fight against slavery. It is this Gospel that inspired heroes like Dietrich Bonhoeffer and Corrie ten Boom to offer Jews refuge during the Holocaust. It is this Gospel that is today fighting against sex slavery and the slaughtering of unborn children in the womb. These movements are made up of individuals who see real injustice and take responsibility, through the power of God, to stop it. Christians do not need "social justice." We have the Word of God as our guide to what causes to care about and how to fight for them.

Without the Bible as our basis for justice, we get a system based on the only tool we have without a supreme moral Law-giver: the self. The best the self can do is a kind of justice based on perception rather than on objective standards of righteousness and truth.

Social justice gives us an overly simplistic worldview of the oppressed versus the oppressor. Applying these categories to all people at all times leads to more unfairness, not less, as adherents aim to reach an impossible outcome of total equality through cosmic calculations that aim to help one group at the expense of another.

Intersectionality-driven social justice reminds us that the world's standards of righteousness are exhausting and elusive. They are arbitrary, confusing, and ineffective. The great news is that Christians have the unchanging God as our guide. Just as we reject the notion of "our truth" in our personal lives, we can dismiss worldly definitions of justice in the sociopolitical realm.

It can be so easy to fall into the trap of believing we have to align with social justice advocates to be considered compassionate and empathetic. We want to be seen as good people, and we'd rather not cause controversy. So we go with the flow. We allow the Twitterverse to direct our outrage, headlines to shape our worldview, and our favorite Instagram influencers to form our morality.

But guess what? We don't have to worry at all whether the world thinks we're compassionate or not. In fact, I can tell you from experience that if you align yourself with the Bible on controversial topics like abortion and marriage, you're going to be labeled a misogynist bigot. People who don't even believe in God will tell you you're going to hell. As hard as that is to take at times, it's okay. There is relief in realizing we don't answer to the rage mob. We answer to Christ, steady, faithful, and sure, who calls us to be set apart and obedient.

While most people build their value system based on what feels good and what's convenient, Christians are called to a higher standard—one that guarantees self-denial and difficulty. That means there will always be tension between us and the world. That's good. We're *supposed* to be uncomfortable here. This isn't our home; heaven is. And as we work to ensure that God's will is done "on earth as it is in heaven," we can expect pushback and persecution.

This is a small price to pay for the freedom and joy of answering to a king higher than earthly authority, whose truth stands firm against the latest cultural dogmas. When we confront confusion, we have clarity in his Word.

The toxic culture of self-love tells us that we are "enough" to determine our own truths. But as we've discussed, this just leads to unsustainable confusion. It's not our or society's truth that matters, it's God's. That's because he's perfect, and we're not.

MYTH #3

YOU'RE PERFECT
THE WAY YOU ARE

THE PARADOX OF PERFECTIONISM

Remember middle school? What a weird time. Everyone is so painfully self-conscious because we don't understand our bodies and we don't know what to do with our hands. These are what I call personality-building years. The cuteness that helped us get our way has faded, and we're forced to develop a sense of humor to make friends and cope with the awkwardness of life.

As girls, we start to want to do things that make us feel older, like wearing makeup or shaving our legs. For me, one of those things was getting my eyebrows waxed. I really wanted to, but my mom wouldn't let me. She said I didn't need it, and she was right. But that didn't stop me from taking a razor from her shower, standing in front of the mirror in my bathroom and slashing one of those babies in half. Immediate regret. And, of course, school pictures were the next day. Not my best.

It's early on in our lives that we women are caught up in what I call the paradox of perfection: hearing and believing we're perfect while simultaneously hearing and believing there's something else we need to do or have (or not do or not have) to *make* us perfect.

Girls are told from a young age by our parents and teachers that we're perfect the way we are. And to some degree, we believe it—even in our awkward middle school years. We're confident that if we could just get our hair to crimp the right way, if our parents would let us wear just a *little* bit of mascara, if we could just get our eyebrows waxed, then maybe—just maybe—we'd finally be able to manifest the beauty and perfection we know is there.

The paradox of perfection follows us throughout our lives, showing up in more profound ways. Today, we most often see it in the online culture of self-love and self-help. In her bestselling book *You Are a Badass*, Jen Sincero writes:

"You are perfect. . . . You are the only you there is and ever will be. I repeat, you are the only you there is and ever will be. Do not deny the world its one and only chance to bask in your brilliance."

Sincero's sentiment is a popular one in this world of trendy narcissism: who you are on the inside—who you *really* are— is perfect. And all you have to do is manifest that perfection, and you'll be happy, successful, and whole.

The "manifesting" is often in the form of things like reading a book, repeating positive mantras, applying certain principles, organizing our belongings, or cleaning up our diet. The paradoxical messages tend to sound something like this:

"You're perfect . . . and this book will help you realize it." "You're perfect . . . and you need to understand your sign to manifest that perfection." "You're perfect . . . and repeating these ten mantras will convince you it's true." "You're perfect . . . and mastering your personality type will prove it."

"You're perfect the way you are" is often a Trojan horse for a product or a program that promises to make our lives better. This means that without these products and programs, it's an empty mantra. If we were perfect just the way we are, we wouldn't need their quick ten steps to make any improvements on ourselves or our lives.

Motivating this paradox is a philosophy that views self-discovery as the road to self-acceptance, or to the actualization of our perfection. Along the road of self-discovery are all kinds of external forces holding us back from realizing, embracing, and manifesting our true perfect self.

Consider these quotes from two popular self-love-centric Instagram accounts:

> "Society has led us to believe our goal is to be beautiful, because according to the white supremacist capitalist patriarchy, beauty = value." @recipesforselflove

"Our dominant culture actively profits from you believing that you are not worthy of love." @emilyonlife

The common theme is that society's standards, social constructs, stigmas, your parents, your boyfriend, capitalism, the patriarchy, mercury in retrograde, and so on are all repressing your true, uninhibited self and are therefore damaging your potential for a great life. If you can just relieve yourself of the unfair burdens these people and systems place on you, you will finally discover your authentic self and find the fulfillment you've been longing for.

From this perspective, you don't have flaws—you have underappreciated qualities. You haven't made mistakes—you've made decisions the "shame culture" wants to guilt you for. You've never failed—you've simply rejected society's unrealistic standards of success.

In *Girl, Stop Apologizing*, Rachel Hollis argues: "For the average woman, the story goes something like this. When you came in to the world you were totally and utterly yourself. It wasn't a conscious decision to be exactly who you were; it was instinct. Then, something changed. Something big happened, something that would shape the rest of your life, even if you have been aware of it at the time. You learned about expectations."

The underlying premise is that who you are deep down is perfect and pure, like a diamond in the rough, and when you chip away at the layers of social norms and arbitrary expectations that have held you back, you'll actualize that reality.

Where's the lie?

First, let's acknowledge what's true about this mind-set. Some expectations are repressive and harmful. You don't have to be a size 2 to be beautiful. You don't have to perfectly balance work and motherhood to "have it all." You don't have to be independently wealthy before you're thirty to be successful. You don't have to be quiet to be kind or loud to be bold. Society shouldn't dictate who you are or what you should do.

You are an individual, which means your life isn't going to look like anyone else's. You have your own talents, your own personality, your own strengths and weaknesses. Some people's criticism of you will be misguided or a result of simply misunderstanding you. These criticisms can be ignored.

Therefore you will have to make hard choices, take responsibility for your own life, and get out of unhealthy relationships.

But none of these things will ever make us perfect because "who we really are" isn't some flawless goddess marred by unfair societal standards or unhealthy relationships.

You are not perfect the way you are, and you never will be.

Scripture reveals this fact to us plainly. Biblically, there are only two kinds of selves: *the old self and the new self.* The old self is enslaved to sin, lost, looking for love and satisfaction in all the wrong places. The old self is totally depraved, hopeless, an enemy of God, and bound for destruction. This is who we all are apart from Christ.

The new self has been redeemed by Christ and is enslaved to goodness, free from the bonds of sin. The new self has everlasting hope, steady joy, and unsurpassed peace because her soul has been saved by God. She is reconciled to him, friends with him, and will spend forever in his presence. The new self has been given a righteousness that's not her own, but one that comes from Jesus.

The new self follows her Maker, understanding that it's not the "universe" that gives her strength and direction, but the God who made it. In his Word, he tells her what is "good, right, and true," and through his Holy Spirit, he empowers her to pursue it. She knows God (Ephesians 5:9) has expectations for her life, and she seeks to meet them: expectations like truthfulness, purity, hard work, generosity, cheerfulness, and self-denial. He has expectations for men and different ones for women. He has expectations for parents and for children, for married people, and for singles.

The new self sees these expectations as good boundaries

set by the Father who loves her, not inhibitions hindering her "true self," because her "true self" is the person God calls her to be, empowered to love him and others and to pursue holiness. This means mistakes and failures and sins do exist. They're not just experiences to learn from, and they're not other people's fault or harmless habits typical of our personality type; they're choices to regret. Not everything taboo needs to be "destigmatized" or "normalized." For the Christian, some behavior has a stigma and is abnormal because God says it should be.

In 2 Corinthians 7, Paul rejoices in a "godly grief" over sin that leads to repentance. Without sadness over sins, we won't be moved to turn from them and realign ourselves with God's will. If God cares about sin so much that he sent his son to die to pay the price for it, we should care about it too. Romans 6 reminds us that God's grace isn't an excuse to sin but is actually the very reason we resist sin.

Obedience to God in all we do is the goal of our lives, which may mean our definition of success doesn't come to fruition. Our call is to do "whatever [we] do, in word or deed . . . in the name of the Lord Jesus, giving thanks to God the Father through him" and to "work heartily as for the Lord, and not for man" (Colossians 3:17, 23).

There is great benefit in creating healthy habits that tend

to lead to a successful life. In fact, the book of Proverbs is replete with warnings against laziness and commendations to work hard, plan for the future, and make wise decisions. These things are for God's glory and our good, but they don't guarantee what the world says is our "best life." They're fruit of the obedience of the new self, not the manifestations of the "best self."

"You're perfect the way you are" leads us into accepting parts of ourselves that we should be rejecting, making excuses for ourselves when we should be repenting, and believing things about ourselves that hold no lasting value.

The toxic culture of self-love is filled with empty platitudes that are handed out not because they're true but because they're profitable and clickable. It makes us feel good to imagine that we're perfect and enough. But, as we've established, we're neither one. And that's okay because God made us needy for his strength and salvation. This is a much better comfort than the delusion that we're flawless.

Even for the Christian women who are aware of our imperfection and need of the Savior, there are still other facets of this "you're perfect the way you are" lie that we need to look out for. Whether we realize it or not, many of us are entranced by the idea that "who we are" deep down inside us is in need of discovery. So we turn to personality tests.

ONE WITH A TWO WING

Every time I've taken the Enneagram test, I've either gotten "one with a two wing" (the "advocate") or an eight (the "challenger"). It used to frustrate me to no end that the result was never consistent.

If you're unfamiliar with it, the Enneagram is a personality test that categorizes people by nine different "types." You can have "wings," which means you have components of two adjacent numbers. So my being a "one with a two wing" means that I am a one, with characteristics of a two.

I got really into the Enneagram in college. A girl who lived on my hall sophomore year talked about it all the time, convincing everyone who'd listen of its accuracy and incredible insight into the human soul. After taking the test myself and getting one with a two wing, I agreed. I bought a couple of books on the test and for years would make everyone I knew take it.

I believed the test had a little more substance than your typical personality tests, and there seemed to be a spiritual component to it, too. I'd even heard that it had been developed by the ancient church by analyzing the nine parts of Jesus's character. To me, it was a beneficial tool to understanding myself and relating to other people that aligned well with our biblical mandate to love other people as we love our-selves.

It wasn't until a few years later that I started to notice the Enneagram's popularity in Christian circles. I saw several ministries and churches selling resources on the Enneagram and even conducting Bible studies and sermon series on the nine types. That's when I started to wonder: Is this healthy?

In his book *The Road Back to You* about the Enneagram, Episcopal priest Ian Morgan Cron writes, "For three years [as a new pastor] I tried everything short of surgery to transform myself into the kind of leader I thought the church needed and wanted me to be, but the project was doomed from the start." Until he discovered the Enneagram, he writes, he felt lost as a pastor, as if he weren't a good fit for the job. After discovering his type, he realized he didn't need to change a thing. He just needed to be "awakened," to know himself better.

Cron asserts that the test is helpful for sanctification. He writes, "Every number on the Enneagram teaches us something about the nature and character of the God who made us. Inside each number is a hidden gift that reveals something about God's heart. So when you are tempted to prosecute yourself for the flaws in your own character, remember that each type is at its core a signpost pointing us to travel toward and embrace an aspect of God's character that we need."

It's this mentality about the test that I began to observe (and grow concerned about) among Christians. This isn't biblical at all. The idea that the God of the universe can be limited by nine man-made personality types is silly at best and blasphemous at worst. The Enneagram isn't our source of knowledge about God; the Bible is. Introspection doesn't take us down a path of sanctification. That's a New Age idea, not a Christian one.

As it turns out, the Enneagram is a relic of New Age philosophy. It was first made known by the early twentieth-century Russian-Armenian mystic philosopher and occultist George Gurdjieff, who believed that humans exist in what he called "waking sleep," and that they can awaken the true, full self by learning the discipline of uniting body, mind, and spirit to achieve a higher consciousness. Gurdjieff and his pupils emphasized the importance of the self: self-actualization, self-betterment, and self-empowerment. His ideas were spread to the West by his own efforts and those of his followers.

It wasn't until later in the twentieth century when another occultist, Oscar Ichaso, and his student Claudio Naranjo developed the Enneagram of personality that was considered a tool for personality analysis with the aim of aiding self-observation and transcendence of suffering. Ichaso claimed that the enneagram was revealed to him by "Metatron, the prince of the archangels" while he was in "some of ecstatic state or trance." Naranjo, who spearheaded the integration of psychotherapy with spirituality and fantasy-enhancing drugs, was a leader in what is known as the "global human potential movement" of the late 1900s, the end goal of which was a life of personal happiness and fulfillment for each individual. In the 1970s, Naranjo's students brought the enneagram to Catholic communities. It is still promoted by a few Catholic leaders today, such as Franciscan friar Richard Rohr, as well as embraced by many evangelical Christians. Yikes!

To constantly focus on our unique attributes is to totally miss the point of what God calls us to do. God calls each of us not to be our "best selves," but to be filled with the fruit of the spirit, which, according to Galatians, is made up of love, joy, peace, patience, kindness, goodness, faithfulness, gentleness, and self-control. We are called to embody all of these qualities, not only the ones that come naturally to us.

Moreover, followers of Jesus know our identity, value, and purpose without taking a personality test. We understand that each of us was made *on* purpose *with* purpose by a Creator who does nothing arbitrarily. Our unique talents and gifts are important and are to be used to help the body of Christ for his glory. Our bodies are dwelling places of the Holy Spirit and therefore are to be in submission to God's will as outlined in his Word. In this sense, we *are* special. We matter.

But Christians also understand that we are depraved sinners in need of a savior. Contrary to the core assumption of self-love culture, we are not good deep down, and nothing we do could ever merit God's mercy. Jesus's followers were "chosen in him before the foundation of the world" (Ephesians 1:4) and therefore can take no credit in our salvation or sanctification. We are irreversibly and eternally secure in him, knowing that "it is God who works in [us], both to will and to work for his good purpose" (Philippians 2:13). We weren't chosen *because* of our good works, but rather *for* good works. No matter how much we introspect, we will never find our good and perfect selves, because they don't exist.

The call for Christians is not to be the best version of their personality type, but to be *like Christ*. No matter what our natural inclinations, strengths, or deficits may be, we are all called to live holy lives. We are all to repent sin. We are all to be obedient. No quirk or characteristic makes us exempt from the standards God has set for us.

Until you realize that the reason you matter is because God created you and sent his Son to die for you, you'll be running a rat race toward the prize of perfectionism that doesn't actually exist. You'll keep trying to be enough for yourself—smart enough, accomplished enough, thin enough, organized enough, and so forth—only to realize sufficiency was never in your nature. It's better to face the facts now: you're going to disappoint yourself.

That we are not called to constant introspection and self-discovery is good news. We can finally be relieved of the duty to constantly search for ourselves. We don't need to search for our purpose or the meaning of our lives. We have worth and our lives matter because *the God who made us says so.*

Unlike the authors of personality tests who don't even know your name, God knew you before time began. He is intimately acquainted with your thoughts, motivations, desires, dreams, what makes you laugh, and what makes you anxious. He wrote every single one of your days before any of them came to be (Psalm 139), and he is with you in each of them. His love for you gives you the comfort you've been needlessly looking for in personality tests and your journey to "find yourself."

The world of self-love tells us that knowing ourselves is essential happiness. We're told that our inner perfection, once found and unleashed, will empower us to succeed and have peace. God tells us something different: that knowing *him* gives us the peace we're looking for and that *his* love gives us the confidence we're looking for.

Once we realize just how not perfect we are, and how little self-discovery contributes to our fulfillment, we begin to see just how unreliable we are as masters of our own fate and rulers of our lives.

This means that rather than follow our hearts, as we're so often encouraged to do, we should question them.

YOUR FEELINGS ARE VALID . . . OR ARE THEY?

I recently came across a post that read "Your feelings are valid . . . all of them. Especially the negative ones." I stopped scrolling and thought about it. Is this true? Are my feelings of anger or jealousy or fear valid?

On the one hand, it's comforting to hear our emotions are justified. There is nothing—and I mean nothing—more aggravating than being told to "calm down" when we're upset. Obviously, if we were able to calm down, we would have taken that option already. No one *tries* to react in a way that's disproportionate to the situation at hand, and even if we do, we don't want to be patronized. We want to hear that our tears or rage or fear is understandable and acceptable.

But is it *true* that all the feelings we have are valid? *Valid* means legitimate, having a basis in logic and fact. I don't know about you, but I've had plenty of feelings that aren't based in reality at all.

I think back to times in high school when I was convinced my parents hated me because I had an eleven o'clock curfew while most of my friends had none. I think of all the times in my life I've been envious of people for being prettier, more accomplished, more fit, more "together." I can easily recall quite a few moments I've been frustrated with my husband for not meeting my (unstated and therefore unrealistic) expectations.

What about the feeling that no matter how much weight you lose, you'll be valuable? What about crippling anxiety that the grades on your exam are going to determine the rest of your life? What about feelings of desperate attachment to the boyfriend who abuses you? What about lust for another woman's husband? What about thoughts of murder or suicide?

Are these feelings valid?

Of course not, because they have no basis in truth. Your value isn't based on your weight. A set of exams can't determine your future. Your abusive boyfriend is bad for you. Another woman's husband isn't yours to want. Nothing in your life will be made better by hurting yourself or someone else.

It's important to distinguish between real and valid. Our feelings may be *real* in that we truly feel them, but they're not valid if they're not based in reality. Our feelings can be very much irrational. If followed, they can send us into a spiral of discouragement and despair. They can lead us to resent people who don't deserve our resentment. They can fill our minds with fear that doesn't need to be there. Worse yet, they can compel us to say or do something that we'll regret and will hurt those around us.

To determine whether our emotions are truly justified, we should ask ourselves a simple question: Why? Why are we upset or fearful? What are we really worried about? What are we actually hurt by?

The other day I was in the car on the phone with my husband. We were talking about a problem I was having at work, and I was off on a passionate diatribe. In the middle of my monologue, he switched from his phone to Bluetooth then asked if I could repeat the last sentence I said.

I was inordinately mad. "Are you serious?" I said (yelled?) before hanging up on him. I fumed for an hour after the conversation and ignored his calls until I got home.

The question I considered hours later was: Was I really upset by the minor inconvenience of having to repeat a sentence? Had he really done anything wrong in switching to Bluetooth? I had to take a deep breath and ask myself: "Why did that make me so mad?"

Once I thought about it, I knew I wasn't really frustrated at him. I was mad at the situation at work. I was stressed out in general. I had three speaking engagements that week plus a deadline for this book, and my patience was thin. I wanted my rant to go uninterrupted, and I had no grace to spare when I was momentarily thrown off course.

My anger toward him was real in the moment, but it wasn't valid, because he hadn't done anything wrong. And because I followed my invalid anger, I lashed out and caused a fight where there didn't need to be one.

While all valid feelings are real, not all real feelings are valid. That means we can *acknowledge* our emotions without *affirming* them. The question of "Why?" can help us determine the difference between valid and invalid feelings. Sometimes we just need to dig a little deeper and realize that we're not being logical. Hanging on to an illogical emotion is only going to make us and those we love feel worse, not better.

The culture of self-love tells us our feelings are valid because deep down we're perfect. Therefore, we can and should trust ourselves. But this is both irrational and unbiblical. As we've already established, we're actually fundamentally flawed, which means our feelings are too.

The Bible is clear that while our capacity for emotion is God-given, feelings aren't to be unconditionally followed. Rather, they're to be bridled by truth and subjected to the authority of Scripture.

The book of Proverbs has a lot to say about ruling our feelings rather than allowing our feelings to rule us. Proverbs 14:29 says this: "Whoever is slow to anger has great understanding, but he who has a hasty temper exalts folly."

How true is that? When we're quick to validate our anger, we often say and do stupid things. Most of us have blurted out something hurtful or harsh in the moment that we didn't really mean. God wants to spare us and those around us from making choices based on our fickle, and at times, invalid feelings.

Sometimes our feelings—not just our outward reactions—are not just illegitimate but also sinful. In Matthew 5, Jesus teaches us that sin starts in the heart. He makes clear that hate and lust are sins, not only the murder and adultery that may follow. In the same chapter, he reminds his followers to let go of anxiety and fear. The ninth commandment God gave Israel was a command against covetousness. Ephesians 4:31 instructs Christians to abandon all "bitterness and wrath and anger and clamor and slander." This means some of our feelings need to be both discounted and *repented* from.

Jeremiah 17:9 warns us that our hearts are "deceitful above all things, and desperately sick." The emotions that flow out of our hearts can be the opposite of valid: they can be based entirely on lies. Why follow a heart that God promises will lead us astray?

Those who worship the god of self have no option but to validate their feelings, because feelings are their only arbiter of what's true. This is exhausting and self-defeating. People eager to agree with every emotion that consumes them are characterized by a lack of commitment, selfishness, and broken relationships because their anger, insecurity, or jealousy continually gets the best of them.

But those who bow down to the God of Scripture know that our emotions don't have the final say in our lives, God does. While our feelings change, God doesn't. Every thought we have is to be held "captive to obey Christ" (2 Corinthians 10:5). This doesn't mean we pretend our emotions don't exist; it means we assess them, examine them, and weigh them against reality and God's Word. We surrender them to our compassionate, attentive Father, who hears us, sees us, and knows what we need before we ask (Matthew 6:8).

The untrustworthy nature of our feelings points to our insufficiency. We're not enough to know which feelings are valid and which ones are going to lead us in the wrong direction.

When we look inside ourselves, we don't find a heart worth following or a perfect goddess worth worshipping. We find an inadequate girl who needs guidance from her Creator. He tells us who we are and in so doing keeps us grounded and steady. Influencers telling us we're beautiful and great will never give us that.

And yet as women we long to be told—even by strangers on the internet—that we're acceptable and attractive. So when we hear the messages of the "body positive" movement telling us to love ourselves as we are, we listen.

BODY POSITIVITY

I gained sixty pounds during my pregnancy. Just a tad over the twenty-five-pound recommendation. It was part baby, part water weight, and a huge part Chick-fil-A. I was never really self-conscious about it, though it wasn't easy watching pregnant bloggers I follow gain a total of, like, eight pounds. But because I enjoy working out, I knew I would get back into the swing of things once she was born. I was fine. Until one day I decided to look at the comments on a Facebook video I'd just posted.

"Okay—there's baby weight, and then there's BABY WEIGHT. Come on."

"Stress can cause people to overeat. It looks like that's what's happened here. Maybe take some time for yourself."

"Wow. You've really gained a lot of weight."

"You're freaking fat."

These are just a few of the comments—verbatim. Until then I'd never cried over something mean said to me online. I've been posting videos of my social and political commentary for almost four years, and I've had my share of hate mail and nasty comments. Sadly, it comes with the territory when you share your opinions with the public. But at seven months pregnant, I was more sensitive than usual. I was aware that I didn't look my best. I was stressed about work, nervous about birth, and anxious about what life would look like when the baby got here. The comments pushed me over the emotional edge, and I crumbled.

I could have sought comfort in the many "body positive" messages strewn across social media that tell me my body is perfect and beautiful no matter what, and that I need to love myself to the point of not caring what people think. And all of that may have eased the pain for a little bit. But I learned through my eating disorder in college that superficial affirmation only goes so far.

So I had to remind myself of deeper truths: God made me and has blessed me with a child, and he's masterfully created my body with the ability to carry her this far. Sure, I could have eaten more salads and worked out more often, but I can't change that now. I have greater tasks before me than obsessing over the comments of strangers. I'm to be the best wife and mom I can be, working hard and remembering where my worth lies.

I truly appreciate how our society has evolved in the representation of different shapes and sizes on social media and advertisements. It's true that a size 2 doesn't have a monopoly on beauty. Though there have been instances of the "body positivity" corner of the internet condoning what appear to be unhealthy lifestyles, I think the new steps toward unphotoshopped and unfiltered depictions of a variety of real women are steps in the right direction.

The problem is the message this movement seeks to convey, which is the lie we've been uncovering this whole chapter: you're perfect the way you are. Again, our perfection is *not* where we find our comfort. And when we try, we end up more insecure and sad than we were before.

Take Angelica's story, for instance.

Angelica's obsessive diet started to consume her life. When she was eight years old, her father passed away, and she grew up with a desperate sense of longing, but for what she wasn't sure. Throughout high school and college, she learned that attention from men satisfied that longing—but only briefly. Falling in love with a man became her goal. "If I wasn't talking to a boy, I literally felt like I was going to die," she said.

She came to believe that if she wanted to find true love, she'd not only need to become beautiful, but she would also need to *believe* that she was beautiful. Insecurity was unattractive, she learned, so she would need to figure out a way to love her body as it was—while also working endlessly to perfect it. "I was told by culture that if I wasn't okay with my looks, and confident in my intellect, and whatever else, I wouldn't be able to have a healthy relationship," she said. "If I didn't love myself in a radical way, then true love wasn't in the cards for me."

She started the keto diet. This time last year she was as thin as she'd been in her whole life. She went on a date with a different boy every week, and by culture's standards, she was "living her best life." What wasn't apparent, however, was the fact that she was drinking herself into oblivion nightly. Despite her physical beauty and the attention she received from men, she was starved for real love—both from herself and others—and the void inside her soul remained.

Our society's only solution for the Angelicas of the world is self-love. If she could just love herself more and care for herself better, if she could think positive thoughts and remind herself of her own greatness, she'll be happy and do great things. If she convinces herself that she's perfect and beautiful and special, she'll be confident enough to stare down her foes.

It's our natural inclination to look for what's going to make us feel better immediately, especially in our culture of purposelessness, individualism, and instant gratification. We want what's going to work, what's going to move us from where we are to where we want to be. And it seems convenient to find that in ourselves—or from other people. Then it's in our control. Then it's just a matter of making a choice and flipping a switch. If the problem is that we hate ourselves, then, of course, the answer is to love ourselves.

But here's the big question: What happens when the self-love runs out? What happens when we look in the mirror and we still don't like what we see? Or how about when we've done something we really are ashamed of? What if we're caught in an unhealthy lifestyle that we feel we can't escape? What happens when the motivational messages and positive mantras and self-affirmation and self-care just aren't enough to give us peace?

Then we're back to the drawing board, wondering why we can't get it together. And in that moment, we don't need to hear that we're perfect the way we are.

Angelica eventually realized, by the grace of God, that placing so much stock in her identity, as successful as it seemed to outside observers, was actually only exacerbating her insecurity and desperation. The skinnier she got, the more she realized being skinny wasn't enough to make her happy. She was trying to love herself as she was, but it wasn't working.

In her book *Love Thy Body*, Nancy Pearcey explains why Angelica's attempts at gaining confidence were failing. "To be obsessed with our body is not to accept it," she writes. The abusive cultural practice of physical self-perfection encourages an "adversarial relationship" with our bodies. Instead, Pearcey reminds us, "our actions should be motivated by the fact that the body is a gift" from God. "We have a stewardship responsibility before God to treat it with care and respect."

Confidence, therefore, is not something to be achieved. It's a gift from God to accept. Unlike confidence derived from the opinions of boys, our female friends, and representations of the "ideal body" on social media, in movies, and in pornography, the gift of God's confidence is permanent and *real*.

This means that, yes, of course we can exercise, lose weight, diet, change our hair and all the rest—but only if we do so in an effort to truly care for the bodies that God has given us. Only in order to glorify him, not in order to worship ourselves. Motivation matters.

The same God who made us is the same yesterday, today, and forever (Hebrews 13:8), and that's the only thing that's rescued me in seasons of self-obsession and moments of self-deprecation. Neither his love nor his plans for his children change based on the numbers on a scale. While we are to steward our bodies responsibly as dwelling places of the Holy Spirit, we aren't obsessed with our appearance, knowing that though "man looks on the outward appearance, the Lord looks on the heart" (1 Corinthians 3:16, 1 Samuel 16:7). We understand that charm and beauty are fleeting, but fearing the Lord is praiseworthy (Proverbs 31:30). So instead of focusing on what we see, we fix our gaze on what is "unseen," because "the things that are seen are transient, but the things that are unseen are eternal" (2 Corinthians 4:18).

Our identity, our significance, and our confidence come

not from what we see in the mirror or what others say online, but from who God is and what he says we are.

Only the one who created us can tell us what we're worth. And he says that we're worth so much that he sent his only Son to die for us, paying for your sins, which are profound and many, so that we could spend forever with him. He did this all for his glory, and for our good. Because of this, we are no longer defined by what we think of ourselves or what others think of us, but who he says that we are.

He says that, in Jesus, you are a new creation. As a new creation, we operate as God calls us to operate: in humility, in love, in forgiveness, in self-control, in diligence, in joy, in mercy, and in justice. As a new creation, we pray for our enemies and bless those who persecute us. As a new creation, we are free from the pressure of fitting in or looking like the rest of the world wants us to look. Who we are meant to be, as followers of Jesus, are self-sacrificial disciples who take God at his Word and are empowered by his Spirit to live in peace and confidence in who Jesus is and what he's done.

These are truths I have to preach to myself often. Every mom knows the pressure of "snapping back" to our prebaby selves, as if the prospect of pregnancy and birth were presented to us without the promise of scars, tears, extra skin, and stretch marks. These are part of the package, which means they're worth thanking God for, not fretting over.

These truths are bigger, better, and longer lasting than the superficial lie that you're perfect the way you are. You're not. None of us is. And that's okay.

Once we let go of the myth of perfection, we have another lie to combat: we're entitled to our dreams.

MYTH #4

YOU'RE ENTITLED TO YOUR DREAMS

DREAM BIG

There's something I haven't shared with you yet: one of the reasons I'm so familiar with the culture of self-love is because I grew up around the closely related culture of self-help.

My parents came from little, got married at nineteen and twenty, and worked hard to make sure they could provide for my brother and me a better life than they'd had. They were both entrepreneurial. As such, they were big on self-development. We listened to leadership tapes, read books on business, and went to motivational conferences and seminars when I was a kid.

And all of these things were a huge benefit to me in many ways. It was through these resources and seminars that I gained my desire to build a career in public speaking. I learned early on how to communicate effectively, how to interact with adults, and how to connect with people in a meaningful way. I also learned the beauty of entrepreneurship from my parents. I saw the perks of working for yourself, and I knew that's what I wanted one day.

But now I see there are some troubling similarities in the self-help world to the toxic culture of self-love. Both say if you do and say the right things, you'll get what you want. In the self-help industry, that typically means career success. Growing up, I just assumed that was guaranteed for me. We talked so much about setting goals and dreaming big in our house, and though I'd seen my parents work hard for these things, I assumed the aspirations I had would just come easily.

I saw a post by the popular athleisure company Spiritual Gangster on Instagram the other day. The tank top in the picture read "You deserve to have everything you want."

Isn't that the message of our day? That our mere existence entitles us to the things we desire—whatever they may be? This is a symptom of the self-centeredness that characterizes our age. Because we serve ourselves, we believe we're entitled to our wants. This is part of thinking we're enough—the more we accomplish, the more self-fulfilled we'll be.

But it's just not true. And because it's not true, it's a mentality that leads to disappointment.

In college, my motto was this: Never turn down a conversation for homework. I stuck to it all four years, and I have no regrets. I (barely) graduated with honors and was even chosen to give the student speech at graduation. Obviously not because I was valedictorian, but it also wasn't based on popularity or extracurricular involvement. I submitted a speech, delivered the speech at an audition, and was chosen. I remember thinking when I delivered the speech: *This is what I want to do for the rest of my life.*

All of this reinforced the idea I'd unknowingly held on to my whole life: *I'll be able to do the things I want to do without having to try too hard.* It was part of the belief in the lie that I was enough. That I was perfect as I was. That my heart was worth following and my "truths" worth manifesting. Though I didn't know what I wanted to do in the long term, I was sure that things would fall into place quickly after graduation. I took a job in PR, which I was sure I would be great at and which would seamlessly lead me into the entrepreneurial life of my dreams.

It wasn't quite that simple."

HUMBLE PIE

When I think back to that first job as a publicist and social media manager, it's hard to comprehend how I was as self-assured as I was. I had never written a press release before. I had no experience in client management. I barely understood how Twitter worked. And yet I was sure I could master the job within weeks.

I remember the first time I realized that wouldn't be the case. It was seven p.m. on a Friday, and I was crying at my desk. My coworker, Monique, looked over helplessly, empathetic but recognizing that I'd gotten myself into this mess, and there was nothing she could really do to get me out.

I'd completely forgotten about a quarterly social media engagement report I was supposed to have completed for a client. I was about three months in, and my higher-up had emailed me that afternoon asking when she could expect the first draft for her review.

When I read the email, I froze. Panic set in. My heart raced, my blood pressure rose. I stared at my computer for a full ten seconds before exhaling. Shoot.

She'd even reminded me about the deadline the week before, and somehow it still slipped my mind. I responded to her email, telling her I'd forgotten but would work on it as quickly as I could. Within seconds of hitting Send, I saw my phone light up on my desk with her name on the screen.

Nothing causes millennials more anxiety than someone answering a text or an email with a phone call. I took a deep breath, walked quickly out the back door that was next to my desk, and answered the phone.

"Hello?" I said, as if I didn't know why she was calling. I don't remember everything that was said in that conversation.

I think I've blocked it from my memory. All I know is that I spent the next thirty minutes in the suffocating Georgia heat listening to her say something along the lines of "You really messed this one up, and I can't trust you." She said that I'd shown incompetence, disorganization, and an inability to manage my time wisely. She was right.

I knew she was right. Still, my feelings were hurt. Was I really this stupid? Surely not. I was better than the person who completely forgets to do an important report despite consistent reminder emails. But, actually, I wasn't.

There was another time I got the date wrong for a catering company that was supposed to cater an event for one of my clients. I called the client at the last minute and asked if he could switch. He emailed my boss and told her I was the least professional person he'd ever worked with in his thirty-year career. Yikes!

Needless to say, it didn't come naturally. There were highs and lows during the two years I worked at that PR firm, but I never did hit my stride. It was hard. I worked late almost every night and still never felt that I came close to mastering my job. Something I should have been good at didn't come easily for the first time in my life.

As hard as that job was for me, I learned a valuable lesson: I'm not entitled to success—even in the areas I typically excel in. I assumed professional success would just happen, and that I'd be fulfilled by my work automatically. I thought I was enough to get what I wanted on my own terms, on my own timeline.

It makes sense that a lot of young people—young women, especially—think the way I did. The #girlboss culture on social media and in the blogosphere makes us feel as if we have to be both obsessed with and totally satisfied by our work in order to achieve any sense of accomplishment in life. All the successful women we follow and read about seem to have found that sweet spot of passion, meaning, and income. We assume that to have a fulfilling life, we have to find it too. In fact, we think we're entitled to it.

But not only is that kind of work not guaranteed, it's also not necessary for work to be meaningful. Though my role as a publicist wasn't my dream job, the work I did at the firm still mattered because I eventually learned to do it adequately and because it met the needs of my clients. I learned that I don't have to love my job for my work to be good and important.

Colossians 3:23 says, "Whatever you do, work heartily, as for the Lord and not for man." We don't have to have the perfect job to glorify God with our work. The work that honors him only has to meet three qualifications: it's *done well*, it *meets a real need*, and it *contributes to the good* of those around us.

This means that whether you're a CPA, a botanist, a janitor, a secretary, or a graphic designer, your work can matter and bring glory to God. Glorifying work doesn't have to earn a paycheck either. Stay-at-home moms, caretakers, and volunteer workers can still fulfill the qualifications for God-honoring work by working diligently to help those around them.

There's a subsection of our generation that believes work isn't inherently important: that we should only be obligated to do what brings us joy, whether it meets a market need or not. The rise of socialism has brought this idea mainstream.

At the 2019 South by Southwest conference, democratic-socialist representative Alexandria Ocasio-Cortez remarked: "We should be excited about automation, because what it could potentially mean is more time educating ourselves, more time creating art, more time investing in and investigating the sciences, more time focused on invention, more time going to space, more time enjoying the world that we live in. . . . But the reason we're not excited by it is because we live in a society where if you don't have a job, you are left to die. And that is, at its core, our problem."

AOC and those who share her mind-set view work as amoral—something we can do but shouldn't have to. This perspective was reflected in the initial summary of her Green

New Deal, which guaranteed "economic security for those who are unwilling to work." The suggestion is that there is no inherent value in working for what we have; thus the government should meet our needs so that we aren't "left to die" if we don't have a job.

This is an unbiblical view of work. God placed Adam in the Garden of Eden to "work it and keep it," before sin entered the world (Genesis 2:15). That means work is not a curse, a consequence of sin, but a *blessing* and *innately good*.

After Adam and Eve sinned, God pronounced a curse on Adam associated with work, that it would be painful and at times fruitless: "Cursed is the ground because of you; in pain you shall eat of it all the days of your life; thorns and thistles shall bring forth for you; by the sweat of your face you shall eat bread."

This tells us two things about the nature of work: humans are meant to do it, but we're not guaranteed success.

Humans were created to reap what we sow and harvest what we cultivate. We are meant to be productive, to contribute our strength, talent, and knowledge to the world in a meaningful way, whether in paid jobs, in volunteer roles, or at home. This gives us dignity and a sense of purpose. The book of Proverbs repeatedly speaks to the importance of diligence and resisting laziness. 2 Thessalonians 3:11–12 warns against the sin of idleness and commends us to work for what we have. We are to steward our earnings as "cheerful giver[s]," as 2 Corinthians 9:7 says, so we can help those who need it. Work is ordained, work is necessary, and work matters.

Those who are physically and mentally able to work but can't or won't find employment suffer not just financially but spiritually and emotionally as well. Our minds atrophy. Our existence begins to feel arbitrary and unnecessary. When we aren't contributing to society, we have the tendency to grow depressed and listless. Human beings need to be needed. Contrary to what AOC and others may say, capitalism didn't make us this way; God did. Good work done well is both for his glory *and* our good.

But because sin has left creation disordered, we are not guaranteed that our efforts will always produce what they deserve. Our investments can flop, our entrepreneurial endeavors can fail, our crops may be ruined, our blogs may never gain traction, and our children may abandon the values that we worked so hard to instill in them when they were in our care. And yet God still commands us to work heartily, not for earthly recognition or success, but for him.

All of this means that work is neither nothing nor everything. Work matters, but it can't forever fulfill us. The self-love culture in which we live simultaneously tells us that we don't need work to have a meaningful life *and* that our jobs are our identity. God's Word says the opposite: work is necessary, but it's not enough to satisfy us. As someone who, after taking a bite of humble pie and learning not everything's going to come easily for me, now has everything in a career I've ever wanted, I know this from experience.

WHEN DREAMS COME TRUE

Today's feminism tells us that a career is necessary to our happiness, but it's just not true. Though I'd started to get the hang of my job at the PR firm about a year in, I never forgot the feeling I had had while standing on the stage at graduation. I knew I was eventually going to be doing something that would put me back on a stage in front of a microphone; I just didn't know what or how.

This was 2015, and the presidential primaries were happening. Though this would be the second presidential election in which I voted, it was the first election in which I was really invested. A lifelong conservative, I was concerned with how our nation had changed over the previous decade. Identity politics and third-wave feminism had run amok, and from my perspective, young voters who leaned left by default were only going to make matters worse. I wondered what would happen if they were more informed about their options. I had an idea.

I was living in Athens, Georgia, at the time, and my husband and I had just got married. I remember telling him what I wanted to do one night on the couch in our old one-bedroom triplex: "I want to tell sorority girls why they should vote in the primaries."

I came up with a nonpartisan presentation on Prezi and started emailing sorority presidents, asking if I could give my presentation at their next chapter meeting. For every sorority that accepted my request, I went.

The value I got out of these presentations wasn't monetary. I got an audience, and more than that, the feeling that I was doing something I was good at. Though I only spoke to a few groups, it was enough to reassure me of what I'd had a hunch about before—that yes, this is what I'm supposed to do.

A few months after I started speaking to sororities, I started a blog titled *The Conservative Millennial*. I was still working full time, and writing about the election was just a hobby. I didn't know where it was headed—if anywhere—but I was having fun, and I had a feeling that I should keep going.

By the end of 2016, I was posting news-centric videos to my blog's Facebook page that were garnering up to hundreds of thousands of views. My husband's job took us to Texas at the beginning of 2017, and it was there that I was offered a job at the conservative media company TheBlaze—but not as a host. I took a job running their social media accounts, knowing that at least having *a* role in the media industry was better than none.

I was soon hired as a contributor, making videos for Facebook and appearing as a guest on its shows. Fox News began booking me on their shows too, and I was continuing to speak locally and regionally to organizations about the importance of engaging young people in politics. In about a year and a half, my hobby had become a career.

In 2018, I started my podcast *Relatable*. My goal was (and is) to provide clarity on culture and the news from a biblical perspective in a way that's easily digestible for women in my generation. I chose the name *Relatable* because I'd learned something in the three years since I'd begun this endeavor: there are a lot of women like me, women who want to know what the Bible says about the chaos that often characterizes our world.

Today I host the podcast, write, speak, and commentate on TV, and for the past year I've had the unbelievable opportunity to write this book. I'm doing everything I've ever wanted to do. I work from home getting paid to do the few things I'm gifted at. There really isn't much that can beat that.

But guess what? As grateful as I am for the privilege of doing what I do, my work still doesn't fulfill me. Political media can be toxic. I've worked hard to keep my distance from the drama that comes part and parcel with this realm, but even day-to-day activity on Twitter is enough to make me wonder if having a career dependent on a public platform is worth it. Having a front row seat to the tribalism that plagues our country and the insanity that seems to characterize our present age can be exceedingly disheartening.

Everything else—the speaking, the podcast, the writing— is all wonderful, but the excitement of them can wax and wane, just like in any other job. Sometimes these things go well; sometimes they don't. I have God-given abilities in these areas, but I also have a lot to learn. There are people in this realm with far more talent; there are also people in this realm with far less talent but who are presented with more opportunities. I've watched godly, honest people be maligned and mistreated while slimy, dishonest people have been elevated. As in any career, many things in this job aren't fair, and success can be fleeting.

When I first started down the media path, I was anxious

about everything. Anxious about Facebook comments. Anxious about followers. Anxious about TV bookings. Anxious about what other commentators thought of me. Anxious about my competition. Anxious to get the opportunities and attention I needed to stay ahead of the game.

Over time, my mentality shifted. There was just no way I could care that much about everything forever; it wasn't sustainable. I settled into a niche that was genuine and meaningful: analyzing culture as a Christian woman. I no longer felt that I had to be caught up on the news every hour, be the first to get my opinion out on Twitter about a recent headline, or post everyday on social media. I'd found the space I wanted to occupy, and I was content to stay there.

In the fall of 2018, we found out I was pregnant, and things came further into focus. I felt in an instant just how secondary a career is to the things that truly matter. Truly, there are no better earthly titles I could hold than "mom" and "wife," as cliché as that may sound. I'd give it all up in a heartbeat for the sake of these two roles.

I *love* what I do. I get to talk with people like you about things that have eternal significance. I honestly can't believe God has allowed me to do so much of what I'm passionate about. But take it from someone who has her dream job: you will get here and realize it's still not enough.

You—your talents, your goal-reaching abilities, your dreams—still aren't enough. If your plan is to make your success your identity, you'll end up empty.

Maybe your dreams have nothing to do with a job. Maybe your dream is to be a wife and mom. While these responsibilities matter immensely and will bring you joy, even these can't fill you completely. No person and no role can replace the longing our Creator alone can meet.

God made us for him, not the other way around. He exists as a king to be worshipped, not a genie who grants us our dreams and wishes. When we follow him, he promises us not to give us everything we want but something far better—himself.

He promises that no matter our job, no matter our salary, no matter our marital status, no matter our fertility or lack thereof, he will be with us. He will be our sustenance, our strength, our joy, our source of satisfaction, our ever-present Help, relentless Redeemer, compassionate Friend, and faithful Father.

In Matthew 6, Jesus urges us not to worry, to resist anxiety, to reject fear in exchange for trust in his provision. If God clothes the lilies of the field in splendor, how much more will he take care of us, people made in his image and children ransomed by the death of his Son? If he was unwilling to spare even his own Son for the sake of our salvation, isn't he trust-worthy to meet the rest of our needs as well?

This is the God our work is meant to glorify. Remember-ing that he is in control and trustworthy frees us from our culture's distorted view of work as either insignificant or iden-tity defining. On both ends of this spectrum there is an under-lying lie: that you are entitled to the life of your dreams, no matter how little or how much work that involves.

God, our authority, says work exists for his glory and our good. He also assures us that though our work won't always be fruitful, he will always be faithful. He doesn't promise that all of our dreams will come true or that our goals will be reached, but instead he commands us to obey him and to work with excellence in whatever realm we occupy. This may include our dream job, and it may not. Either way, we can have peace knowing we're able to fulfill our aim of glorifying him no matter what role we fill.

MYTH #5

YOU CAN'T LOVE OTHERS UNTIL YOU LOVE YOURSELF

ME FIRST

"The bottom line is that you can't love others if you don't love yourself first," writes Victoria Osteen, wife of megachurch pastor Joel Osteen. Her husband has preached the same: "If you don't love yourself in the right way, you can't love your neighbor. You can't be as good as you are supposed to be."

According to the Osteens, God's love empowers us to love ourselves, which enables us to obey Jesus's command to love our neighbors. Self-love is possible only if we first love ourselves.

The Osteens are simply reiterating an idea that's been popular in Christian circles for decades. In the 1970s, books like *Love Yourself* by Walter Trobisch, a German pastor, and *The Art of Learning to Love Yourself* by Cecil Osborne, a Baptist minister, were published by Christian publishers. These books argued from both a theological and a psychological perspective that self-esteem and self-acceptance play crucial roles in Christian life in that they determine how well we can love other people.

Author Jen Hatmaker makes the same argument in her book *For the Love*: "We love people the way we love ourselves, and if we're not good enough, then no one is." These Christian leaders echo the sentiment of singer Miley Cyrus, who expressed it best in an interview with *Elle* about her marriage to Liam Hemsworth: "Why are we trained that love means putting yourself second and those you love first? If you love yourself, then what? You come first." It's worth noting that, sadly, their marriage dissolved in less than a year.

According to this line of thought, loving ourselves is a prerequisite to loving those around us. That gives us a good (even a biblical-sounding) excuse to focus on ourselves before and instead of focusing on the wants and needs of others. The reasoning claims its roots are in Jesus's central command to love our neighbors *as ourselves*. If we don't first love ourselves well, then the love we give other people won't be good either.

But Cyrus understands something self-love promoters in Christian-ish circles aren't willing to admit: to commit to self-love is actually to commit to selfishness. Whereas Cyrus and her secular cohorts regard selfishness as a virtue, followers of Jesus do not.

Jesus's command to love others as we love ourselves is not a command to love ourselves. "[A]s you love yourselves" assumes self-love, because Jesus, who created us, knows self-love is innate. This doesn't mean we look in the mirror and always like what we see, or that we consider ourselves talented or likable. In fact, we can think horrible things about ourselves and still be practicing self-love. The love that we were born feeling for ourselves isn't romantic or affectionate but is a love that looks out for our best interests. As Blaise Pascal explains in his 250th Pensé, "All men seek happiness without exception. . . . It is the motive of all actions of all men, even of those who contemplate suicide."

We are born looking out for our well-being. Those who harm themselves and end their own lives are still looking out for their own interest, as they're seeking a way to alleviate their pain. Meeting our own needs comes more naturally to us than anything else in life.

Self-love shows up not just as an innate drive for self-gratification and self-preservation but also as self-justification. Not only will we do whatever possible to meet our own basic needs, we also insist upon seeing ourselves in the best light possible. As C. S. Lewis points out *The Weight of Glory*: "In our own case we accept excuses too easily; in other people's we do not accept them easily enough."

We're quick to justify our actions, even while condemning the same action done by others. That's how fiercely—and blindly—we love ourselves.

I know what you're thinking: but what about the people who really hate themselves? The kids who blame themselves for their parents' divorce? The woman who thinks her boyfriend's abuse is her fault? What about the girl who picks herself apart every morning when she looks in the mirror? Don't they need a crash course in self-love?

It's true that these people have unhealthy views of themselves and may be wrestling with self-loathing. That's who I was in college, as I was attempting to rebound from rejection by starving myself and downing Crystal Light and vodka four nights a week. I was looking for satisfaction and affirmation and love in all the wrong places. I looked like a case study in self-hatred.

And I *did* hate things about myself. I *was* insecure. I *did* feel inadequate. But I never stopped loving myself. I was living the life I was living because I thought it would make me feel better. Even in my self-consciousness and loneliness and insecurity, I never stopped considering my best interest. I was just wrong about what my best interests actually were.

Frankly, I was self-obsessed. I was constantly thinking about what I deserved, wondering "why me?" and looking for new ways to make myself feel better. Self-obsession and self-hatred aren't mutually exclusive. Most of the time they go hand in hand. This is a hard to admit but universal fact of human nature.

We don't have a self-love deficit in this country—or anywhere. We never have. Despite how insistently psychologists for the past half century have told us that the key to better behavior and more satisfying lives is higher self-esteem, the research—even in secular circles—just doesn't hold up.

In 2002, Lauren Slater wrote a piece for *The New York Times* titled "The Trouble with Self-Esteem." In it she highlights the failures of decades of theory that have asserted that the higher view we have of ourselves, the more responsible and fulfilled we'll be. She says this:

"It has not been much disputed, until recently, that high self-esteem—defined quite simply as liking yourself a lot, holding a positive opinion of your actions and capacities—is essential to well-being and that its opposite is responsible for crime and substance abuse and prostitution and murder and rape and even terrorism."

But this simply isn't the case. Slater continues:

"In 1986, the State Legislature of California founded the Task Force to Promote Self-Esteem and Personal and Social Responsibility. It was galvanized by Assemblyman John Vasconcellos, who fervently believed that by raising his citizens' self-concepts, he could divert drug abuse and all sorts of other social ills. It didn't work. In fact, crime rates and substance abuse rates are still formidable, right along with our self-assessment scores on paper and pencil tests."

Slater cites Nicholas Emler of the London School of Economics, whose research found that "there is absolutely no evidence that low self-esteem is particularly harmful, and that people with low self-esteem seem to do just as well in life as people with high self-esteem." Researcher Roy Baumeister of Case Western Reserve University found that "low self-esteem is in most cases a socially benign if not beneficent condition but also that its opposite, high self-regard, can maim and even kill."

If we're honest, we're a little offended by their findings. You're telling me that it's okay—better, even—for me not to think of myself highly? Not to think I'm beautiful or talented or strong or full of potential?

Our minds have so intertwined self-affirmation and success that we're afraid that if we stop telling ourselves how great we are, our lives will take a nosedive into misery. We'll start to wallow in self-pity, our relationships will grow toxic and codependent, and we'll fail at work because we'll be crippled by our own self-doubt.

But that fear ignores the reality that as Christians, our options aren't boiled down to high self-esteem versus low self-esteem, or self-love versus self-hatred. We choose neither. Instead, we operate out of total self-forgetfulness.

Tim Keller illustrates this truth in his book, *The Freedom of Self-Forgetfulness*. In it he explains that "the essence of gospel-humility is not thinking more of myself or thinking less of myself, it is thinking of myself less." I love how he describes what this looks like:

> Gospel-humility is not needing to think about myself. Not needing to connect things with myself. It is an end to thoughts such as, "I'm in this room with these people, does that make me look good? Do I want to be here?" True gospel-humility means I stop connecting every experience, every conversation, with myself. In fact, I stop thinking about myself. The freedom of self-forgetfulness. The blessed rest that only self-forgetfulness brings.

Blessed rest indeed. Depending on our own self-esteem for healthy relationships or lifelong fulfillment is exhausting because it depends on a variety of factors that change every day: our job performance, our weight, our popularity, our mood, or our ability to think good things about ourselves. Instead, we choose self-forgetfulness, and we replace our self-love with God's love, which is dependent on a factor that will never change: our salvation in Christ. Contradicting everything our culture tells us, it turns out the prerequisite for real love is self-forgetfulness, not self-love.

And what a relief this is. Because of Jesus, we have an answer to our insecurities, our self-criticism and self-doubt, and it's *so much better* than flimsy, shallow self-love. Our answer is *him*, the eternal, unchanging Creator and Sustainer of the universe, who paid for our sins on the cross, declaring us forever forgiven, innocent and righteous before a just and holy God. What deeper and surer confidence could we ask for than to be irrevocably purchased by Jesus's perfect sacrifice, not as a reward for our goodness but as a gift by his grace?

This same Jesus calls us not to self-love but to self-denial and full obedience. He doesn't tell us to learn to love ourselves before we love other people, because his love for us is more than sufficient to equip us to love those around us.

Philippians 2:3–4 says, "Do nothing from selfish ambition or conceit, but in humility count others more significant than yourselves. Let each of you look not only to his own interests, but also to the interests of others."

That is the kind of love Jesus is calling us to when he tells us to love our neighbors. As we look after our own needs, look after theirs. As we seek our own interests, seek their interests. As we fight for self-preservation and self-justification, be quick to make provision for them, and give them the same benefit of the doubt you give yourself.

The love we show our neighbor may not manifest as affectionate feelings, because there are times we may not feel affection for them. Love of neighbor is about applying the same instincts we have to take care of and be kind to ourselves to other people as well.

This will mean, as the Philippians 2 verse says, counting others as even more important than we count ourselves, and sacrificing our needs for the good of others. I first learned what this looked like in high school.

YOU DON'T HAVE TO WAIT

The love that we, as Christians, show people—as unlovable as they may be—is a reflection of God's love for us. We, too, are unlovable. We, too, are undeserving of God's approval and affection. And yet even while we were yet sinners, God made a way through Christ to have a relationship with us (Romans 5:8). We don't have the right to ignore or dismiss people because they're hard to love, because God didn't dismiss or ignore us.

That means we are free to love people *right now*, rather than waiting until we have positive feelings toward ourselves. When we put off loving other people because it's hard or we think we need to commit to self-improvement first, three things happen: we disobey God by ignoring people's needs, people's needs go unmet, and we miss out on life-giving, empathy-building experiences that make us more like Christ. I learned this for the first time in high school.

My older brother, Daniel, is on the autism spectrum. He is kind, funny, a lover of history, and a treasure trove of random facts. He's also had a difficult life.

Daniel has always been on the outside looking in. Making friends has never come naturally to him, no matter how hard he's tried. Growing up, my other brother and I attended the same school, but Daniel never could. While we had places to go, people to see, and normal teenage challenges to face, Daniel never knew what it was like to be "in." He still doesn't.

When I was little, I would pray that God would make him "normal." I didn't understand why he didn't talk like everyone else, why he couldn't read well, or why he went to a different school. As I matured, I realized "normal" wasn't a goal Daniel would or should ever aspire to. His differences are exactly what make him who he is—gentle spirited, brutally honest, and curious.

God has used Daniel to help me take notice of other people like him. The summer after my junior year of high school, my church took a group of students to a camp for people with special needs called Camp Barnabas. For a few days of the year, campers whose disabilities range from severe to minimal are able to do things "typical" people get to do on a daily basis: swim, go down slides, go camping, play sports, and hang out with people who look and act like them. As volunteers, we each served as a camper's "buddy" for the week. We stayed by their side all week to ensure their experience at camp was the best it could be. It was the hardest, most rewarding experience I'd ever had, and I was in love.

The next year, I spent six weeks at Camp Barnabas as a staff member, coleading a cabin of campers and volunteers. It's hard to describe the exhaustion and joy that comes with caring for so many women with such a wide variety of spiritual, emotional, and physical needs. Feeding, bathing, comforting, holding, helping, encouraging, and loving people who could do nothing for us in return required a level of sacrifice I hadn't reached until that point. Self-denial was the mode of operation, and self-forgetfulness was the norm.

I think back to my seventeen- and eighteen-year-old self, and I see, in most ways, a typical teenager. I was a self-focused, moody, insecure girl who just wanted her boyfriend to love her and for her parents to leave her alone. But God was working on me, and he used Camp Barnabas to show me who he was.

Though I was raised in a Christian home, I didn't have a personal relationship with Christ until I was a junior in high school. I had a Bible teacher who challenged us to ask hard questions about God and to dig into Scripture for the answers. He led discussions and debates that sparked my interest in who Jesus is and what following him would look like. I started reading C. S. Lewis, and his book *Mere Christianity* made faith seem more real to me than it ever had.

I stopped going to the church I was raised in and switched to a church of my choosing. It was this church that led me to Camp Barnabas, where I learned what it was like to be Jesus's hands and feet. If I'd waited until I loved myself enough to love other people, I would have missed out on the opportunity to love and serve people as Jesus loves and serves us.

Believing the lie that we have to love ourselves before we love other people will cause us to miss out on the most joyful experiences of our lives. And even more important, there are people whose needs won't be met because we're too busy meeting our own needs to pay attention to theirs.

I think of all the campers at Camp Barnabas, many of whom had never had a real friend. Some of them will never know what it's like to be invited to a party, to have a job, or to get married. They are dependent on their parents for everything—eating, going to the bathroom, getting dressed. Imagine what would happen if their caretakers suddenly decided they needed to focus on themselves instead of spending so much time with people who can't give them anything in return?

I think of Daniel, who will likely always struggle with fitting in. And I think of the people who have taken the time to get to know him even though he's shy, who have had a conversation with him even though he can be hard to talk to, and who have loved him even though he doesn't always know how to show love back. Daniel has been ignored, rejected, put down, and excluded more than most of us have. I don't want to think of a world in which the people who have loved him so well chose not to because they needed to work on themselves first.

Consider all the souls untouched and mouths unfed if missionaries tried to find the perfect balance of self-love before they helped other people. Consider the lives unsaved and the freedoms unprotected if soldiers waited until they could celebrate their flaws before they laid their lives on the line. Consider all the people without shelter or sustenance if volunteers at homeless facilities decided they needed to work on their self-esteem before they could lend a hand to those who need it.

The people who suffer from our narcissism are the most vulnerable. The idea that "you can't love other people until you love yourself" reeks of entitlement and elitism. While we're busy trying to come to terms with cellulite on our thighs, there are people who are desperately hurting, lonely, and in need of our love and care.

That we have to wait until we love ourselves to love other people like this is a lie from the pit of hell. Satan would love nothing more than for us to waste our time with fleeting efforts in self-betterment while people around us are suffering. Jesus shows us a better way.

He gives us an example of what it means to love others as ourselves through the parable of the Good Samaritan. A Samaritan helps a Jewish man who was robbed and left for dead on the side of the road. Unlike the priest and the Levite who passed the victim by, the Samaritan took the time to help him, bind his wounds, and pay for his stay at a local inn.

The key context of this passage is that at this point in history, Jews and Samaritans hated each other. That means the love demonstrated by the Samaritan isn't one of admiration, it's one of determination. It's the kind of love we would naturally show to ourselves even when we look in the mirror and don't like what we see. It's one defined by kindness, protection, and preservation.

As C. S. Lewis says, "Love is not an affectionate feeling, but a steady wish for the loved person's good as far as it can be obtained."

We can see this steadfast love demonstrated by Christians whose sacrifices have weighed far more than mine. Christians are the most persecuted religious group throughout the world. In Syria, China, North Korea, India, and elsewhere, Christians are silenced, imprisoned, tortured, and martyred for practicing their faith. Martyred missionaries like Dietrich Bonhoeffer and Jim Elliot are examples of the kind of radical love Christ requires of his followers.

Christlike doesn't always look like physical martyrdom. My aunts, who live in Arkansas, have both dedicated their lives to ministering to the poor and the homeless in their communities, helping them obtain food, clothing, transportation, and helping them get jobs. Local Christian pregnancy centers do incredible work for moms and their babies, not just offering free pregnancy and STD tests and ultrasounds, but many also offer parenting classes, affordable clothing, and other resources to help families start off on the right foot.

Anytime we deny our own wants, needs, and priorities to show kindness and share Christ with someone else, we glorify God. And not only do we not have to wait until we've accomplished self-love to do it, helping others even when we feel our worst fosters a joy that self-absorption can't give.

I'll be the first to admit I fail at this often. I choose selfishness. I choose convenience. I choose to love myself more than I love other people. I'm greedy with my time and stingy with my energy. I want comfort, safety, and happiness. I don't want to expend too much for other people at the risk of feeling burned out.

It's so easy to get caught up in the busyness of our own lives and forget that there are others who desperately need our love, time, and resources. But this selfishness is a sin we need to repent of. In a day when people are literally dying of loneliness, Christians have the responsibility to offer a love that can save lives—both now and forever.

Maybe this means volunteering at church or a local non-profit, maybe feeding the homeless, maybe coming up with a solution to a problem you see in your community. Or maybe it means something more drastic: joining the on-the-ground fight against sex slavery or teaching skills to women in Kenya. These are endeavors in which God can be trusted to lead you as you pray and seek wisdom from the godly people around you.

If you're a mom (especially a mom of babies, like me), you may not have time to start a nonprofit or even spend an afternoon volunteering. Same goes for students and caretakers and those of you whose "nine-to-five" all but consumes your life. As we talked about in the chapter on work, what we do on a day-to-day basis can also be used to love others and share the Gospel.

Romans 12:2 calls our bodies a "living sacrifice." This means that our whole lives are meant to be dedicated to God in worship, not just certain compartments. Being a mom or student or employee who does our work with joy and excellence for the glory of God and the good of others is also an act of Spirit-filled generosity.

We are to take every opportunity to be generous with our time and energy and money on behalf of the people God places on our path—those in loneliness, destitution, and lostness—and we're to do so with the express purpose of showing them Jesus Christ and leading them to the well that never runs dry.

Prioritizing self-love over love for those around you doesn't just affect your generosity toward the people who need your help; it also affects your most important relationships.

THIS IS SO MUCH BETTER

One of the reasons young people are waiting so long to get married today is because we've been convinced that we have to do all the things we want to do before we get there. We want to love ourselves, find ourselves, and know ourselves before we can truly give ourselves to someone else. But, honestly, this is a waste of time. Explicitly avoiding marriage for the sake of self-discovery does nothing more than defer the joy that's found in building a life with someone you're committed to.

I met my husband, Timothy, in September 2014, shortly after I'd begun recovering from my eating disorder and rampant partying. I was in a good place: I was happy being single, figuring out life in a new city, and I'd decided to start a new workout routine. I'd joined a CrossFit-type gym outside of Athens, and that's where I saw him for the first time.

I don't remember very much about my first impression. He was cute and in shape, and that's all I noticed. We were both in the 5:30 p.m. classes on the weekdays, and after a couple weeks he struck up a conversation. Small talk eventually led to afterworkout chats, which eventually led to lingering discussions in the parking lot. One night, after several weeks of conversation after class, we talked in the parking lot for four and a half hours! It was then that we realized we probably should just go on a date.

After that long parking lot conversation I texted a friend and said, "I think I've found my husband." She thought I was crazy, and I honestly did too. I remember hearing married people say when I was in high school and college that "when you know, you know." I didn't believe them. How do you just *know*? Aren't there a million things to think about before you make a decision like that? I don't know how to explain it, but they were right. I just knew. Five months later we were engaged. Four months after that we were married.

We didn't wait until we loved ourselves to choose to love each other. We were imperfect, grateful, and sure. This timeline certainly isn't right for everyone, but it worked for us, and we haven't looked back.

Before I get into what I've learned in marriage and how it's taught me about self-sacrificial love, I want to take a second to give you some practical dating/engagement advice. This stuff is based on what I've learned through my experiences, and I don't have a Bible verse to attach to every line. But I know how confusing relationships can be, especially when you're trying to figure out whether to marry the object of your affection, so I'm going to give you the best advice I know in the hope that it will add clarity to your own dating life.

First of all, if you're a Christian, your spouse needs to be a Christian too. And not just an I-was-raised-going-to-church Christian. If you're serious about becoming more like Christ, he needs to be serious about it too. The goal of your dating relationship, whether it lasts or not, should be to bring you closer to Jesus. While no guy and no relationship is perfect, both of you should be working to make this a priority both individually and together. This point alone covers a lot of bases.

Second, you need to like him. I know this sounds obvious, but believe it or not, there are many Christians who don't think this is important. I was one of them! I remember hearing a sermon in college that said singles were being too picky with their spouses and just needed to pick a Christian and go for it.

And yes, unrealistic standards may leave you needlessly miserable. Arbitrary characteristics like eye color will probably need to go to the wayside. But you absolutely should be attracted to—both physically and emotionally—the person you're with. This is the wonderful part of living in the West in the twenty-first century: we have options, and we get to enjoy the benefits of God-given romantic love and attraction.

One thing I love about Timothy is that we make each other laugh. He thinks I'm clever, and I think he's funny even when he's not trying to be. I also love how we can have deep, satisfying conversations. These have always been the things that have drawn me to him.

It's not selfish to ask yourself if the person you're dating makes you happy. I mean, it certainly sounds like the lovers in the Song of Solomon were enjoying themselves. This doesn't mean your boyfriend worships the ground you walk on and never makes a mistake or even makes you happy *all the time*. But—are you happy to be in his company? Can you be bored together and still enjoy each other's presence? Do you want to spend time with him after one of you goes home? Can you see yourself with him forever?

If the answer is no to any of these questions, you should ask yourself: Why are you still with him?

You may be afraid of a few things: that no one is going to love you as much as he does, that you're never going to find someone as good as he is, or that you won't know how to function as a single woman. Maybe you've been through a lot together, and you just can't imagine starting over with someone new.

I've feared these things too, and I can tell you from experience that *none of them* is a good enough reason to stay with him. Fear isn't a good justification for getting married.

Here's what I've told more young women than I can count: *you should not be convincing yourself you want to be with him.* Likewise, you shouldn't have to persuade *him* to be with you.

If you're in this kind of relationship, it may mean you're making an idol of dating or marriage. If you're willing to be miserable just because you don't want to be alone or deal with the pain of a breakup, there could be something much deeper going on in your heart than incompatibility with your boyfriend.

The sense of assurance I had with my husband was a huge difference from what I felt with the person I thought I was going to marry in college, the one who met all my qualifications on paper but about whom I had nagging doubts from the beginning. Feelings aren't everything, but they are *something*, especially if they're giving you warning signs that something's not right.

Don't ignore the pressing into your gut that tells you your boyfriend or fiancé isn't right for you. If you're with them out of fear, that means you may be hanging on to an idol that you need to let go of.

And when you do let go, it'll hurt. That doesn't mean you didn't do the right thing. Do what I wish I'd done after my college breakup: be patient as God heals you. Pray, meditate on Scripture, remind yourself of his promises. Go to church and be with friends who will lead you to the cross, where Jesus, the bearer of burdens, will take your weighty baggage and give you rest.

I can't promise that God has your future husband waiting around the corner, or even at all. God doesn't promise us earthly blessings in exchange for obedience. He promises us a peace, a joy, and a deep contentment that far surpasses any happiness an earthly relationship could bring.

The seventh chapter of First Corinthians describes singleness as a gift because those who have it are undistracted from the troubles that come with marriage and are able to fully devote themselves to the Lord. Christians who remain single aren't "missing out"; they are offered the same satisfaction in Christ as those who are married, and, bonus: they have the time and capacity to do things married folk can't. As big of a fan as I am of marriage, it's important to me that all of you reading who want to be married and haven't found a guy to lock it down yet know: marriage is *not* the goal of the Christian life. It is not when our "real life" begins. Your real life began when you decided to follow Jesus, and, because of his commitment to lead you down a path for his glory and your good, you have everything to look forward to. Marriage is one of many ways Christians may be called to sacrifice. But nothing's stopping you from loving the people in your life today.

Of course God directed me toward marriage, and I am thankful he did. When our relationship started, we were like most couples who fall in love quickly. We couldn't get enough of being together. Every spare second was spent either in each other's presence or on the phone. We sent long emails to each other at work. We wrote letters. Being apart was physically painful. When I hugged him, I felt like I could never hold him long enough. I knew marriage was the only way to satisfy what felt like an unquenchable love for him.

And, as it turns out, it was. Marriage turned out to be all I'd hoped it would be and more. I got to come home to my favorite person every day, eat food together, and watch Netflix. For all the talk of marriage being a trap, I'd never felt freer or had more fun.

I still feel this way. Almost five years into marriage, I still couldn't ask for anything more. But that doesn't mean it's been easy.

I heard a saying once as a teenager that I've now learned to be true: marriage is a four-letter word, and it's not love—it's work. *Work* is the best word to describe this past year of our lives.

Everything in our lives, including our marriage, shifted when we welcomed our first baby in July. We went from focusing on each other to giving all our attention to this child who'd so drastically captured our hearts. For those first few survival-mode weeks, we barely had a conversation. When we did talk, it was in frustration or disagreement. He was overwhelmed, I felt underappreciated, and neither of us had the energy to communicate our feelings. Instead of hashing it out, we let the tension grow.

More major life events happened: we moved houses and both of our grandmothers died all within a span of two months. Pulled in a million different directions, we started to grow apart. The rare quiet moments together in the evenings were spent on our phones and computers with the TV on in the background. We'd get in daily, petty fights because one of us nagged the other or overreacted about a change in plans. There was always tension when we were in the same room, and we knew we could easily erupt in an argument if the other so much as stepped in the wrong direction. We were stressed, and instead of helping each other, we were tearing each other down. We were far apart in the same home.

Seasons like this are when commitment isn't fun anymore, love isn't natural, and conversation isn't easy. Gone are the dating days when you couldn't get enough of each other. Now it's an effort to spend more than fifteen minutes together without fighting. This is when you're required to make a choice to either deny yourself and love when you don't feel like it, or do.

The culture of self-love tells us life's too short to stay in a marriage that doesn't make us happy. As a post on the self-love account @femalecollective argues: "Reminder: relationships are supposed to make you feel good." That logic makes sense only if the self is the highest priority. But if everyone really thought that way, we'd all end up alone.

My husband and I held on to each other through a tense season of marriage by reminding ourselves and each other that even when this doesn't feel good, we're in it for the long haul. We chose to forgive when we wanted to hold a grudge. I chose to bite my tongue when I wanted to criticize. He chose to say sorry when he wanted to defend himself. These are things we're still practicing every day.

We're only in the beginning of our life together, and we're by no means experts on marriage. Fortunately, we both have parents who have modeled marriage well, and we're able to take wisdom from people who are ahead of us. This is wisdom we've gleaned not just from our own experiences but from the experiences of people who have endured far more. We've known marriages that have survived deaths of children, bankruptcy, infertility, chronic illness, and even infidelity. We understand that surviving every level of trial in marriage requires a laying down of ourselves for the sake of the other.

A question you may be wondering is: Why? Why stay in a marriage that doesn't always feel good? I can give you both a practical and a profound answer. First, for the practical.

A study published in *The Atlantic* by General Social Survey in April 2019 showed that "married young adults are about 75 percent more likely to report that they are very happy, compared with their peers who are not married." A 2019 Pew Research study reports that married people are also happier than unmarried couples who live together. A 2018 study by Dr. Paul Amato found that marriage quality improves for couples who stay together through discord.

All marriages go through rough patches and seasons of serious challenges. Even so, couples who fight through them and stay married typically have a greater chance of happiness than those who don't or those who are unmarried. The happiness that comes with marriage isn't always a feeling but rather an abiding contentment knowing that you're part of the team that will stick together through the troubles life brings.

But there's a much more profound and important reason to get and stay married, and it's that marriage reflects Christ and the church. Because of that, a strong, Christ-centered marriage paints a picture of the Gospel to the world.

In Ephesians 5, husbands are called to love their wives as Christ loves the church, and wives are called to submit to their husbands as they submit to the Lord. In this way, husbands and wives are engaged in mutual and constant self-sacrifice that reflects the good news of Jesus's sacrifice on the cross and his commitment to his church. Marriage serves as an earthly depiction of the eternal reality of God's redemption of his people through his Son.

Though the world will call the Christian model of marriage outdated and oppressive, those who are in this kind of relationship know the benefits of security and unconditional love are far better than unreliable, unfulfilling self-love.

Christian marriage reminds us continually that we're not enough—not for ourselves or for each other—and that God alone gives us our satisfaction and our strength to hang on when being together feels more like work than romance.

My humble advice: if you can, get married. And now. If you're with the person you know you want to marry, go ahead and do it. Don't wait until you graduate, until you have enough money, until you've traveled more, until you've lived more of your life single, until you get your promotion. If you're engaged, don't draw out your engagement. Yes, there may be real circumstances keeping you from getting married right away, but if there's any way to rectify these circumstances so that you can say "I do," don't wait.

By waiting, you're opening yourself up to getting closer to sex before marriage and wasting precious time you could be spending figuring out life together rather than separately. Just as you don't have to love yourself before you love other people, your ducks don't have to be in a row before you get married. Line them up together. It's way more fun that way.

If you want to get married but haven't found the person, please don't lose heart. You will get married one day or you won't, and either way, Jesus and his promises to be faithful to you and sustain you don't lessen or change. The lessons of self-sacrifice and the joy found in generous love are for you to be enjoyed as much as they are for anyone. Enjoy the community of people with whom God has surrounded you. Be where godly people are. Invest in friendships, share your wisdom, obey God's voice, and revel in the precious reality that your responsibility is to him alone.

MOTHERHOOD

If there's one thing that pulls us out of our self-absorption even more than marriage, it's being a parent.

As I write this, our six-month-old baby girl is sleeping in the room next to me. For those of you who are parents, you know what a whirlwind this newborn stage is. In a blink of an eye, your universe shifts. You realize you didn't know what it meant to be tired or stressed before this. You start to forget what life was like before becoming a mom. What was it like to go to the bathroom or take a shower in peace? Do regular people finish meals? Will I ever drink a whole cup of coffee without having to microwave it sixty-seven times before nine a.m.?

Every single decision you make—from when you'll go to the bathroom to what you'll eat for lunch—is centered on the well-being of this child you've just brought into the world. Your entire schedule revolves around naps, feedings, baths, diaper changes, and playtime, even as you're working or meeting other obligations. You can't wait for them to go to sleep, but you miss them when they do, spending that precious hour of quiet staring at the monitor instead of checking off your to-do list.

I remember the day I found out I was pregnant. I had one test left under my sink, and I decided to take it, because why not? We'd been trying to no avail for five months and I was conditioned to disappointment, but it was around that time, so I went for it. I took the test, set it on the counter, then changed into my workout clothes. After a few minutes, I walked by to pick up the test and instinctively headed toward the trash can. Then I saw that fateful word on the screen: "Pregnant." *What?* I was doubled over in disbelief. I was going to be a mom! And nothing's been the same since.

I can be a pretty anxious person, and that was exacerbated times a million when I got pregnant. All of the things that were completely out of my control hit me at once. What if I have a miscarriage? What if I take a really hot bath and accidentally melt the baby? What if I'm sick for the next nine months, and I can't do my job? What about birth? Can I give birth? Am I capable of that? Oh, my gosh, I hate hospitals; what if I have a mean nurse? What if something happens to Timothy or me? We're all going to die, aren't we?

I was constantly coming to terms with my own insufficiency—my inability to predict the future, to control the outcomes, to ultimately ensure the baby's health and our safety. So much was completely beyond my grasp for the first time, and I learned in a new way what it meant to be not enough.

During birth, some of my fears were realized. Though I hoped and prayed and planned for an all-natural birth, that's not what went down. At forty weeks and six days, I had a "failed" induction that led to a C-section, which was an outcome I'd never even entertained. My husband and I were both terrified. I was disappointed in myself, exhausted, anxious, crying, and shaking uncontrollably as they wheeled me into the operating room. This was not at all what I'd planned.

But it's true what they say: none of that matters once they lay that sweet baby on your chest. Lying on the operating table with Timothy next to me, numb from the waist down and clueless to how the procedure was progressing, I heard the doctor say, "Hi!" Then, as if in response to her first greeting, baby girl let out a loud scream—the best sound I'd ever heard. They lowered the curtain in front of me, and showed me my wide-eyed, crazy-haired, seven-pound, ten-ounce precious daughter.

After that, I was changed.

Everything that was once big now seemed so small. And you know, in that moment, you would do anything—anything at all—for this child. You would stop at nothing to protect her and make her feel loved.

It's a unique kind of love. A profound, unconditional, heartbreaking love that you've never known. It's as if a giant tidal wave hits you and you realize—oh, so *this* is what God's love for me is like. *Now* I'm starting to understand the kind of love that compelled him to send his only Son to die on a cross for us.

I have very little time, if any, to myself these days. I'm literally writing this at two a.m. because I can only find a quiet moment in the middle of the night. My daughter requires more of me than I ever could have imagined. And I'm not enough—that much is painfully true. I can't be everything she or anyone in my life needs. I'm at more than full capacity at almost all times.

And yet I wouldn't trade it for anything. I wouldn't trade the sleepless nights, the diapers, the total lack of free time, for the world. God has humbled me relentlessly through motherhood, continually bringing me to my knees as I ask for things I can't give her myself. I've never wanted so much that I can't provide for someone. I want her to know truth, to be wise, to be healthy, to be strong, to be protected from those who wish to do her harm.

I can only do so much to bring these things to fruition so most of my time is spent surrendering. Surrendering my anxious thoughts, my fears, my plans, and my aspirations. And I'm not good at it. I like being in control. But pregnancy and birth and motherhood have taught me more poignantly than anything else that control is ultimately a myth. God is making me okay with that. He is teaching me to trust him more than I've ever had to.

There's no question motherhood is hard. It is. Let me say, though, not just as a first-time mom but also as someone who knows moms who have way more kids than I do, who knows moms of special needs kids, who knows moms whose life as a mother has been exceedingly trying, it's worth it. It is so incredibly worth it.

I am troubled by the stories of how our generation doesn't want kids. A 2019 NBC poll showed that only 30 percent of Generation Z and millennials think having children is very important. BirthStrike is an organization discouraging procreation in the name of combating climate change, and they're echoed by other antinatalists arguing for a hold on birthing babies. *Full Surrogacy Now: Feminism Against Family* is, believe it or not, a book that people are actually reading that proposes a complete obliteration of "natural motherhood" in exchange for paid surrogacy in an effort to break apart the nuclear family. Some people are against having kids because they just think the world's too scary. Some people just don't want to be weighed down or inconvenienced.

Vice published an article analyzing this phenomenon in

2019. The author, Hannah Ewens, noted: "[N]one of my friends in their late twenties talk openly about hopes of having a baby; rather, we flinch when we see a child walking around, out in public, on its hind legs. It's a furry friend we want. One that'll love us, not drain our minimum finances and not get in the way too much."

This makes sense in light of what we know about many in our generation, considering how little sacrifice is required by pets in comparison to babies. Not only do they require less supervision, they also demand nothing of us emotionally. We don't have to let go of our bad habits and hang-ups. We don't have to mature. We don't have to learn how to communicate effectively or set a good example for them. If we're consumed by the culture of self-love and committed to worshipping the god of self, we don't want to be put off by the demands of a child.

Here's a hot take on that: the intense love many young nonparents feel for their pets is probably just an expression of their natural biological instinct to care for a child. I think about the shift that happened in our own lives when our baby was born. As much as my husband and I love our pets, they were both quickly relegated to second fiddle when we brought our daughter home. Though I insisted while I was pregnant that that wouldn't be the case, I never could have guessed that the love we felt the second our baby came into the world would be so all consuming. While our pets are still well cared for, their significance to us doesn't come within light-years of our love for our daughter.

And that's how it *should be*. Humans, especially *our* humans, should be more valuable to us than animals. Not only because people are uniquely made in God's image, but also because he *made us* to need human relationships—intimate family relationships—not just companionship with our pets. Christians have an obligation to demonstrate to the world the special value of human beings and specifically of children.

Abortion culture is rampant, as organizations like Planned Parenthood and NARAL work tirelessly to sanitize and even glorify the procedure that kills a defenseless baby, renaming it "freedom" and "choice." Their language, propagated by a leftist-dominated media, perpetuated in schools and strewn across social media, has influenced a generation of young girls to believe that the life inside them that they helped create is nothing more than a parasite to be discarded as they please.

That's why I think how we talk about motherhood, how we think about motherhood, and how we act as mothers matters. Motherhood is hard, but it is good. It's a gift that we have the privilege of stewarding. As much as we can, our attitudes should reflect that, especially when we're talking about being a mom to other people. Avoid toxic online mom culture that calls kids and toddlers brats and burdens. It may be sarcasm, but it has an effect on how people see parenting and family. Let Christian moms be the first ones to say: "No, as hard as this is, my baby is a blessing, not a burden."

I don't want to sound preachy or self-righteous by telling you how we should talk about our kids. I know I'm a new mom, and some of the struggles of having multiple kids or kids with special needs are unfamiliar to me. But I *am* familiar with both how mainstream culture speaks negatively about children and how, by contrast, God instructs us to view them: as a heritage for which we should be grateful rather than obligations we dread (Psalm 127:3). That doesn't mean we can't say when it's hard and ask for help—we should, absolutely. But our prevailing message to the world about motherhood should be one of gratitude, not grumbling.

In a culture of self-love that's convincing women that they need to love themselves before they can love other people, our cheerfulness as moms tells a different story: that there is joy in pouring yourself out, even when you don't feel filled up. That sacrifice is worth it. That even though we're not enough, that's okay because God is.

My practical advice to you regarding motherhood is similar to my advice regarding marriage: if you can, do it. My husband and I did what many of you are probably doing: planning and waiting for the right moment. There is certainly wisdom in preparing for the future and creating as much security and stability for your child as possible. But if you're putting off kids because you're just not ready for that kind of commitment, I'll tell you what someone probably should have told me two years ago: it's time to grow up. It's time to ask God to help your emotional maturity match your biological reality.

If you are a mentally stable and physically able married adult woman, you are ready to have children. Don't buy into the secular nonsense that "adulting" doesn't happen until you're thirty-five and that not knowing how to do adult things well into your twenties is normal. It's not. Our culture extends adolescence *way* too long, and as Christians who want to honor God's design for marriage and the family, we should take joy in being adults and having responsibility. That doesn't mean that paying bills or changing diapers at three a.m. is always fun, but we understand that these obligations are the good parts of growing up, and we accept them and thank God for them.

I know many women who would love nothing more than to become moms but haven't been able to. They've either suffered miscarriages or struggled for years with infertility. They would trade anything to have pregnancy pains or late night feedings. They'd love nothing more than to take this next step of marriage and adulthood, but they don't know whether it's ever going to happen for them. They feel hopeless. If that's you, know that God is with you. He is for you; he is sanctifying you and teaching you; and you have no less value to him because you do not have a child. In Christ are all we need for love and contentment and joy. You are a Christ follower first—that is your defining and highest purpose. Any other title that comes along—or doesn't—is secondary.

It's a relief to know that I don't have to wait until I meet an arbitrary standard of self-love before I can love other people. How would I ever know that I've finally loved myself enough to finally form relationships, have children, or help those around me? Know that you don't have to wait either. God's love is all you need for confidence and the ability to love others.

You're not enough for your own fulfillment. God made you not only to need him but also to need other people. Popular culture will tell you to invest only in relationships that feel good and help you advance your goals. God tells us that sacrificial love *is* the goal.

Our culture's fixation on self-love isn't working. A 2019 *Forbes* article titled "Millennials and the Loneliness Epidemic" analyzed a study by *The Economist* and the Kaiser Family Foundation that found that 22 percent of adults in the United States "always or often feel lonely or isolated." The piece notes that prior to the 1960s, single-person households were rare, but now that share has doubled, exceeding the number of households of married couples with minor kids. Another study found that 46 percent of women are more scared of loneliness than of a cancer diagnosis.

Couple young people's loneliness with rising rates of depression and anxiety, and it's obvious that whatever tactics the world is offering us to ease our pain and gain confidence aren't cutting it. Young people are putting off getting married and having kids; they're opting out of church; they're sucked into their devices and enslaved by their jobs, all in an effort of self-discovery; and they're still ending up lonely and discontented.

Waiting to love yourself before you love other people will only lead you down a path of selfishness that leads to a dead end of loneliness and misery. It's God's ever-replenishing love that gives us all we need to care for those around us (1 John 4:19).

While "the thief comes only to steal and kill and destroy" in the name of self-love, Jesus came that we may have abundant life through him (John 10:10). His way leads to joy, to peace, to wisdom, to comfort, to steadiness, to purpose—to all the things you've been told to look for in yourself but haven't been able to find.

You're not enough. You've never been enough. You never *will be* enough. And that's okay.

CONCLUSION

What I've learned over the years is this: the seasons defined by self-centeredness have been my most miserable, and the times in my life when I have felt peace and fulfillment have been the moments when I've removed myself from the center, reoriented myself around God and his truth, and remembered that I'm not enough.

Camp Barnabas, my discovery of the wisdom of the Bible in high school, my turning away from a lifestyle that was killing me and reminding myself of the truths I'd learned years earlier and had since abandoned, my marriage to my husband, and learning to be a mother to my daughter: these are the seasons and the things that have brought contentment. And not a single one of them came without sacrifice. Each of them was marked by denying my sufficiency, succumbing to my own inadequacy, and turning to God to tell me what's true. Without him, I'd have ended up in the ditch of my own making.

My years as a selfish teenager, my recklessness during and

after my last semester of college, and my refusal to let go of an addiction I knew wasn't good for me were all a result of making myself my own god.

Placing ourselves in the center of our universes always leads us to confusion and chaos. It convinces us of our "enoughness" and leaves us disappointed when our sufficiency inevitably proves a mirage. It makes us feel we have the authority to determine our own truths, only for us to realize we're unable to distinguish right from wrong on our own. It encourages us to chase after perfection—both within and outside of us—leaving us exhausted when we see that perfection was just a mirage. It tells us that our dreams are ours to have, that we deserve everything we want, leaving us bitter when we don't get our way. It assures us we can only love other people when we love ourselves, ensuring we end up alone.

Getting to a destination is impossible without a map, and the same is true for life. Without directions, we're aimlessly wandering, looking for love and fulfillment in places that can't give them to us. The only adequate guide is the God who made us, and through his Word he shows us truth and righteousness, and in his Son, Jesus, we find purpose for both this life and the next.

The call of those who follow this Jesus isn't one of self-love or self-affirmation, but self-denial. Jesus asks his disciples to take up their crosses and follow him. He is not a genie waiting to fulfill our wishes. He is not a cheerleader standing on the sidelines of the game of life. He is Lord. The Great I Am. Our Creator, Sustainer, Reconciler, and Hope. He is a King to be worshipped and a Leader to be followed. He does not exist for us, but we exist for him. He is counter to what the world offers us in self-absorption and fleeting happiness, and he's so much better.

It is through the self-forgetfulness found in Christ and the humility of following his commands that we find life—nowhere else. When we recognize him as God, removing ourselves from the center, we find the "enoughness" we've been craving.

It's not found in ourselves. We are not enough, and we were never meant to be. That's good news.

ACKNOWLEDGMENTS

I'm incredibly grateful to the Lord for his unrelenting faithfulness and goodness, and I'm thankful he gave me the opportunity to write this book.

Everything I do is propelled by the love and encouragement of my husband, Timothy. He keeps me grounded and lifts me up. And so does our baby, whom I'd just like to thank for being so cute.

Thank you to my parents, who laid an excellent foundation for me growing up and who continue to be my best advice givers and biggest cheerleaders. They and the rest of my family—my brothers and my in-laws—are all in my "balcony," and I'm so glad to have their support.

Immense thanks to my book agent, Maura Teitelbaum, for being so good at what she does and such a pleasure to work with.

I can't show enough appreciation to the wonderful Helen Healey at Sentinel, who believed in me from the start, who tracked with me through a million different ideas and changes, who gave me grace when I missed my deadlines (which was often), who sympathized with the demands of pregnancy and then of being a new mom, and who offered me clarity and encouragement when I needed it. When I say this book wouldn't have happened without her, I mean that literally.

Thank you to the whole Sentinel team, who have been working hard behind the scenes for a long time to make this book happen. You guys are the best.

I'm thankful for the help of Glenna Whitley, who patiently yet persistently helped me shape my often-rambling ideas into actual chapters.

Thank you to Charles Dorris, my speaking agent, who has effectively helped me make the most of the opportunities that have come my way for the past few years.

Thanks to Blaze Media, which distributes my podcast, *Relatable*. The show has become the light of my professional life.

And last, thank you to the readers, especially those who have been with me for years, who followed my blog and who listen to the podcast. I've always said I have the best audience in the world, and it's true. Everything I write, every speech I give, and every podcast I put out is for you guys. Your support means so much.